The

"If you read one book this year, make it this one. Christian higher education is only excellent when the faculty who serve students looks like the students Christian universities are committed to admitting and graduating. Presidents, provosts, deans, and college trustees will find *The Hispanic Faculty Experience* a treasure. Read it today."

—**Shirley V. Hoogstra**, president, Council
for Christian Colleges & Universities

"Here is an essential work for all those ministering in Christian higher education to hear the voices of Hispanic professors in shaping our shared future."

—**Robert W. Pazmiño**, Valeria Stone Professor of Christian Education,
emeritus, Andover Newton Seminary at Yale Divinity School

"This anthology brings a seasoned, informed, and thoughtful group of Latina/o scholars and educators to share eloquently about their joys and pains, their struggles and achievements, and their sacrifices and victories in following a personal and Christian vocation in predominantly white schools within the orbit of Christian colleges and universities."

—**Luis R. Rivera-Rodríguez**, vice president,
Hispanic Association for Theological Education

"Mirroring the diversity of Latine in the United States, this collection of stories allows all readers to truly understand their Hispanic colleagues' doubts, frustrations, commitments, and dreams. A must-read for senior administrators seeking to increase the number of students, faculty, and staff among their ranks."

—**Alvin Padilla**, professor of New Testament; dean, Latino and Global
Ministries at Gordon-Conwell Theological Seminary

"Latine people as well as non-Latine people will gather wisdom, grace, and love from the offering of the gifts of these lives. Read only if you are ready."

—**Elizabeth Conde-Frazier**, director,
Association for Hispanic Theological Education

"It is incumbent upon White culture to remember Hispanics not as a current trend in new enrollments but as a population overlooked and underserved for decades. The authors challenge us to mentor the next generation of young faculty, especially those from minority backgrounds, toward success, an opportunity too important to ignore."

—**James R. Moore**, director of accreditation, Association of Theological Schools

"This book is the first to focus exclusively on the Hispanic faculty experience. I trust these voices to shepherd Christian colleges and universities into the increasingly diverse and hopeful future that God has in store."

—**Robert Chao Romero**, author of *Brown Church: Five Centuries of Latina/o Social Justice, Theology, and Identity*

"Drs. Esqueda and Espinoza provide faculty and administrators with a clearer understanding of the Hispanic leaders' narrative and how that narrative is to be heard in the border context."

—**Mark Maddix**, dean, School of Theology and Christian Ministry, Point Loma Nazarene University

"Timely. Necessary. Affirming. Through the powerful use of stories, each essay in this volume creates a window to the various and often overlooked experiences of Latina/o faculty in Christian higher education. *The Hispanic Faculty Experience* is a critical resource for understanding the Latina/o faculty experience in the United States."

—**Norlan Hernández**, director, Jesse Miranda Center, Vanguard University

"*The Hispanic Faculty Experience* is full of tears, frustrations, joys, and sincere moments of vocational questioning. All authors are *valientes* (courageous) and an example of a faithful *testimonio* (testimony) that the Holy Spirit sustains in each step of the journey."

—**Oscar Merlo**, director, Center for the Study of the Work and Ministry of the Holy Spirit Today, Biola University

"This book is especially valuable to executive leadership in education, who are invested and committed to diversity, inclusion, and equity and are making them an integral component of their educational culture. The educational life journeys of the scholar's stories represented in *The Hispanic Faculty Experience* will help the reader see many blind spots in our educational systems and in cultural understandings."

—**Joanne Rodríguez**, executive director, Hispanic Theological Initiative

THE
HISPANIC
FACULTY
EXPERIENCE

THE
HISPANIC
FACULTY
EXPERIENCE

OPPORTUNITIES FOR GROWTH
AND RETENTION IN CHRISTIAN
COLLEGES AND UNIVERSITIES

Edited by
OCTAVIO J. ESQUEDA
and BENJAMIN D. ESPINOZA

Abilene Christian University Press

The Hispanic Faculty Experience
Opportunities for Growth and Retention in Christian Colleges and Universities

Copyright © 2023 by Octavio J. Esqueda and Benjamin D. Espinoza

ISBN 978-1-68426-229-8

Printed in the United States of America

Library of Congress Control Number: 2023938988

Cover design by Faceout Studio
Interior text design by Scribe Inc.

For information contact:
Abilene Christian University Press
ACU Box 29138
Abilene, Texas 79699
1-877-816-4455
www.acupressbooks.com

23 24 25 26 27 28 / 7 6 5 4 3 2 1

Contents

THE IMPORTANCE OF OUR VOICES IN THE ACADEMY

Octavio J. Esqueda

¡Estamos aquí para quedarnos! (We are here to stay!) Hispanics do not represent a current trend in the United States or higher education. We have been here for centuries and embody an integral part of the nation. As President Joe Biden's nominee as education secretary, Dr. Miguel Cardona, said in 2021, "And I, being bilingual and bicultural, am as American as apple pie and rice and beans."[1] Hispanics personify the mixed fabric of this nation. Therefore, Hispanics are not newcomers or a recent development that the country in general, and Christian higher education institutions in particular, are now discovering as the new reality they must address. We have been here, but others have not completely seen us until now that they need us because traditional enrollment is decreasing, causing financial distress to most institutions.

Who are we? In the United States, different terms attempt to describe us: Hispanic, Latino/a, and more recently, Latinx and Latine. There is no consensus about the best term, and all of them are imperfect and problematic. In Latin America and other areas of the world, people use nationalities to refer to themselves. In the United States, the tendency is to group people from different nationalities into one representing diverse backgrounds, cultures, and in some cases, languages. This practice erases the identities of people, primarily non-White, because it reinforces their minority or perceived permanent foreign status while Whites are considered just "Americans" or the normative group.

For this reason, any attempt to classify diverse people with one term presents limitations, as if one single story could encompass a myriad of multiple stories. As the novelist Chimamanda Ngozi Adichie masterfully explained in her famous TED talk, "The Danger of a Single Story," "The single story creates stereotypes, and the problem with stereotypes is not that they are untrue, but that they are incomplete. They make one story become the only story."[2]

Hispanic is the oldest and most widely used term for us in the United States. This term relates to Spanish-speaking people or descendants of Spanish-speaking countries. Hispanics (*hispanos*) are those whose heritage is connected to Spain and its colonies regardless of their Spanish proficiency. Most institutions have traditionally used Hispanic as the common term, and because of its popularity and acceptance, this book also uses Hispanic as the preferred term. Two main limitations of the term Hispanic are the impossibility of specifying gender and the heritage exclusion of Brazil and other non-Spanish-speaking countries in Latin America.

For this reason, the term *Latino* and the feminine form *Latina* became popular in the United States. *Latino* provides the Spanish flexibility to add gender and plurality: Latino/a/os/as. However, these variables may need to be clarified for the reader and complicate the spelling of the term for the desire to include both genders in both singular and plural. In primarily academic circles in the United States, *Latinx* emerged as an alternative that moves away from the gender dualism of masculine and feminine and offers a gender-neutral option. This term, however, is rare among Hispanics in the United States, and it is completely foreign to people in Latin America. The English enunciation of "x" of Latinx makes it unpronounceable in Spanish. Therefore, in some recent academic circles, the term *Latine* has become a better alternative to *Latinx* because it demonstrates gender neutrality and corrects the English pronunciations of *Latinx*. This book acknowledges the differences between authors and the difficulty of using a term that encompasses all people and their preferences. Therefore, even though we, as editors, use *Hispanic* as the general term in the book, all contributors had the liberty to use the term of their preference. You will notice this difference as you read the distinctive book chapters.

Christian colleges and universities are increasingly interested in becoming Hispanic-Serving Institutions (HSIs). This government category applies to not-for-profit, degree-granting higher education institutions where Hispanic students make up at least 25 percent of enrollment.[3] A few theological institutions have established Hispanic programs and initiatives for decades, while many evangelical theological seminaries have just recently started Spanish programs. A primary focus of these institutions is the potential Hispanic students can have to increase their enrollment and impact. Still, at the same time, they ignore the past circumstances that alienated Hispanics and other minorities. For this reason, in some instances, it may seem that Hispanics and minorities are needed but not necessarily wanted. There is a need for an honest introspection that hopefully leads Christian higher education institutions to focus their reaching efforts based on theological convictions instead of merely economic and pragmatic motivations. Sharan Merriam and Laura Bierema describe well the current reality of higher education in the United States: "Embedded in this convergence of demographics, economics, and technology is a value system based on the political and economic structure of capitalism . . . with the shift to a consumer approach to higher education, the institution worries about its 'brand' appeal, its profitability, its 'share' of the market . . . the decreased importance of individuals in the new market economy in observing that humans as resources take precedence over humans as humans beings."[4] In the literature and practice, there have been minimal efforts to explore how the Hispanic professoriate can facilitate these institutional initiatives to reach and serve Hispanics better. One notable exception is Peter Rios's *Untold Stories: The Latinx Leadership Experience in Higher Education*. This book fills this void in the literature and practice by exploring Hispanic professors' career paths in Christian higher education.

Most are aware of the gap between the desire to serve Hispanics and how significant their underrepresentation is in Christian higher education. The following section presents a visual overview of Hispanics in the United States, in higher education, and in the Council of Christian Colleges and Universities (CCCU) and the Association of Theological Schools (ATS). These numbers highlight the enormous need for a fair representation of Hispanic students and, more notoriously, Hispanic faculty.

Numbers and Hispanic Representation in General, Higher Education, CCCU, and ATS

In General

- The US Hispanic population reached 62.5 million in 2021, up from 50.5 million in 2010. Hispanics made up nearly one in five people in the United States (19 percent). Hispanics became the largest racial group in California in 2014 and in Texas in 2021.
- People of Mexican origin accounted for 59.5 percent (about 37.2 million) of the nation's overall Hispanic population in 2021. Those of Puerto Rican origin are the next largest group, with 5.8 million.
- Four in five Hispanics are US citizens (80 percent). The share of US Hispanics who are immigrants is on the decline and varies by origin group.

Higher Education

- The number of Hispanics in college is 4.1 million. The share of Hispanics in college increased from 14 percent in 2010 to 19 percent in 2021. Women represent a higher share of Hispanic students, with 56 percent for 46 percent of men (this gender gap is present with all racial groups).[5]
- In the fall of 2020, of the 1.5 million faculty at degree-granting postsecondary institutions, 56 percent were full time, and 44 percent were part time. Scholars of color are much more likely to be assistant professors than full professors.[6]

Rank	People of Color (%)	White People (%)
Professor	22	78
Associate Professor	28	72
Assistant Professor	36	64
Instructor	29	71
Lecturer	27	73
Nonacademic Rank	25	75

- The full-time faculty numbers for Hispanics and minorities are staggering, according to the National Center for Educational Statistics:

      39 percent White males

      35 percent White females

      7 percent Asian / Pacific Islander males

      5 percent Asian / Pacific Islander females

      3 percent Hispanic males

      3 percent Hispanic females

      3 percent Black males

      4 percent Black females

      1 percent or less for Indigenous American / Alaska Native

- Only 2 percent of full professors are Hispanic males and 2 percent are Hispanic females, and 3 percent of assistant professors are Hispanic males or females.

Council for Christian Colleges and Universities (CCCU) Institutions

- In 2018–2019, they had 454,821 students:

      58.5 percent White

      11.3 percent Hispanic

      10.8 percent Black

      4 percent Asian / Pacific Islander

      0.5 percent Indigenous American / Alaska Native

- In 2018–2019, they had 15,117 faculty members:

      83.8 percent White

      2.9 percent Hispanic

      4.4 percent Black

      4.6 percent Asian / Pacific Islander

      0.3 percent Indigenous American / Alaska Native

- In 2018–19, they had 6,775 administrators (full and part time):

      84.4 percent White

      4.1 percent Hispanic

      5.2 percent Black

      3.1 percent Asian / Pacific Islander

      0.3 percent Indigenous American / Alaska Native[7]

Association of Theological Schools (ATS) Institutions[8]

- In 2020–21, they had 76,635 students: 50,199 male and 27,879 female. They had 5,790 Hispanic students: 3,940 were male, and 1,828 were female.

- In 2020–21, they had 2,279 male professors (1,668 White) and 800 female professors (522 White).
- There were 113 Hispanic male professors and 37 Hispanic female professors.

Professor	36 (males)	9 (females)
Associate Professor	47 (males)	5 (females)
Assistant Professor	25 (males)	17 (females)
Others	5 (males)	6 (females)

The Importance of Personal Stories

An African proverb says, "Until the lion learns how to write, every story will glorify the hunter." This book provides the much-needed and unique opportunity for Hispanic faculty members in CCCU institutions to share their experiences as professors in predominantly White institutions and encourage the next generation of Hispanic scholars coming through the ranks. In this book, we use the framework presented in *The Cruciform Faculty: The Making of a Christian Professor* about the roles and duties of Christian professors (teaching, research, service, and mentoring).[9] All chapters tell the stories of Hispanic faculty members from their own voices with a general framework of their career to the professoriate and their experiences in teaching, research, service, and mentoring.

Each chapter, however, is different in tone and style. This situation is intentional with the desire to demonstrate Hispanic professors' common challenges and yet different experiences in Christian higher education settings. Although all authors are Hispanic, they represent various backgrounds, denominations, and locations. Their ages, academic disciplines, career paths, and levels of faculty seniority also vary, but together they bring a beautiful mosaic of Hispanic voices to the academy.

This book is a collection of personal stories. Our stories exhibit a testimony of perseverance and determination amid many difficulties. We dared to become vulnerable not because of personal vindication or, even worse, as a desire for "self-victimization." As I (Octavio) typed those words, the words of a senior colleague came back vividly to my mind. We were members of an important search committee at our institution. As we reviewed CVs and discussed possible candidates, this distinguished professor made a strong racial comment that surprised me. He said it would be helpful to have a smart Black scholar around to change his perspective about Blacks because, in his experience, this group was uneducated and uncultured. I intervened and said that the comment was not appropriate and failed to represent minorities who constantly face discrimination and other challenges. He responded that what I described was inaccurate and that minorities only enjoy "self-victimization." His comment shocked me, but the silence of my colleagues—including two deans, one of whom was the only other person of color in the room—surprised me even more. No one dared to contradict this senior colleague. To this day, I frequently reflect on how someone can actually "enjoy" being a victim. We guarantee you that this book would be unnecessary if the career paths of Hispanic professors were accessible and without racial obstacles or difficulties.

Why, then, do we share our stories? We do it as a gift to others, as a gift to you. We decided to open our hearts to illustrate what it means to be a Hispanic faculty member in Christian settings. We invite you to walk with us in our journeys through the professoriate. We welcome you into our pain and joys, into our failures and accomplishments, and into our vocation as Christian educators. Welcome!

Notes

1 Erika L. Green, "Biden's Pick Confirmed as Education Secretary," *New York Times*, March 1, 2021, https://www.nytimes.com/2021/03/01/us/politics/education-secretary-confirmed.html.

2 Chimamanda Ngozi Adichie, "The Danger of a Single Story," TEDGlobal, Oxford, UK, October 2009, 19:16.

3 For more information about HSIs, see this excellent book: Gina Ann Garcia, *Becoming Hispanic-Serving Institutions: Opportunities for Colleges and Universities* (Baltimore: Johns Hopkins University Press, 2019).

4 Sharan B. Merriam and Laura Bierema, *Adult Learning: Linking Theory and Practice* (San Francisco: Jossey-Bass, 2014), 22–23.

5 This information is drawn from an analysis of US census data. See Jens Manuel Krogstad, Jeffrey S. Passel, and Luis Noe-Bustamante, "Key Facts about U.S. Latinos for National Hispanic Heritage Month," Pew Research Center, September 23, 2022.

6 "Characteristics of Postsecondary Faculty," US Department of Education, Institute for Educational Sciences, National Center for Education Statistics, May 2022, https://nces.ed.gov/programs/coe/indicator/csc.

7 Council for Christian Colleges and Universities, "Diversity within the CCCU," *Advance*, Spring 2020, https://www.cccu.org/magazine/diversity-within-cccu/.

8 Association of Theological Schools, "Table 3.1: A Number of Full-Time Faculty by Race/Ethnicity, Rank, and Gender—All Schools, 2020–2021," *Annual Data Tables*, https://www.ats.edu/files/galleries/2020-2021_Annual_Data_Tables.pdf.

9 Mark H. Heinemann et al., *The Cruciform Faculty: The Making of a Christian Professor* (Charlotte: Information Age, 2017).

1

TEACHING AS A CALLING

Thriving and Surviving as a Mexican
(and American) Professor

Octavio J. Esqueda

I "blame" my Sunday school teacher, Fernando Amezcua, for my becoming
a seminary professor. I was twelve years old when he asked me to teach
our Sunday school class once a month. To this day, I am amazed he would
delegate the Sunday lesson about the book of Romans to a young man like
me. I asked him about it recently, and he said he saw potential in me and
that we can only grow if we receive an opportunity to do it. Fernando and his
wife, Luz María, have been excellent mentors and encouragers for most of
my life. Professors exist for the students, and our calling is always connected
to our service to others. We indeed "teach who we are and whose we are,"
as the great educators Parker Palmer and Robert Pazmiño have indicated.[1]

In addition to my teaching involvement in my congregation, where I
was in charge of the youth Bible study, I began my professional teaching
career when I was nineteen at a public middle school in México. When I was
twenty-two, I also started teaching at Colegio Guadalajara, an important
private high school. I taught my first college class at twenty-four at ITESO
University (Instituto Tecnológico y de Estudios Superiores de Occidente),
a prestigious Jesuit university in Guadalajara. I am not a faculty member
because of external circumstances or as a second career, but I am incredibly
fortunate to be a professor because it has been my life's calling.

However, my initial career as a Spanish and literature professor changed after I taught my first Bible class when I was a student at a seminary in Dallas, Texas. I confirmed then that I enjoyed teaching about God, and it reaffirmed my desire to become a professor in a Christian higher education setting. I knew I needed a doctorate, so I pursued a PhD in higher education at the University of North Texas. At that time, this public university had a collaboration agreement with Dallas Theological Seminary that allowed me to transfer my minor in Christian education from the seminary. Dr. Barry Lumsden, the professor from UNT who made this agreement possible, later would become my mentor and dissertation chair. Dr. Michael Lawson, the Christian education department chair at DTS, became my mentor and dissertation committee member. Dr. John Plotts was my third dissertation committee member, and the three played vital roles in my life and teaching career. They supported me and believed in me not only through my studies but also as I looked for teaching opportunities after I completed my doctorate at thirty years old.

I have shared elsewhere my journey between completing my doctorate in the summer of 2003 and becoming a professor at Southwestern Baptist Theological Seminary in January 2004.[2] This institution was established in 1908 in Fort Worth, Texas, and I became the first Mexican-born professor in its history. After teaching there for over seven years, my family and I moved to Southern California so I could teach at the Talbot School of Theology at Biola University. Interestingly, Biola was also established in 1908, and (to my knowledge) I'm also the first Mexican-born and -raised professor to teach at Talbot and probably the whole university. Although these institutions are located in Texas and California, where the Hispanic population is predominantly of Mexican origin, they reflect the national tendency of underrepresenting faculty members of Mexican origin. Therefore, I have been one of the few Hispanic voices on campus and the only one representing Mexicans in these theological institutions for twenty years.

I used to be the youngest teacher everywhere I taught, but things have changed. I am now a tenured full professor of Christian higher education and director of the PhD and EdD programs. I have had the opportunity to teach in several countries on different academic levels. Teaching is my passion and my calling. In the same way, I also enjoy academic leadership primarily because it allows me to empower others to flourish in their own callings. I had a few mentors as a student, but for most of my teaching career, I have felt alone and without mentors, especially Hispanic mentors. While I was a student in the United States, I never had a Hispanic or minority faculty member. As a Hispanic professor in predominantly White institutions, I also had to learn to navigate the professoriate life alone. My current institution has zero Hispanic representation in senior and midlevel administration, and I am the highest-ranked Hispanic faculty member. Therefore, I literally have no role models to imitate or mentors to guide me.

For this reason, at this stage of my academic career, I intentionally seek ways to mentor and guide younger faculty members, especially from minority backgrounds. The professoriate tends to be a lonely life with limited opportunities for collaboration. This book hopes to empower the voices of Hispanic faculty members who, for the most part, navigate alone in their institutions. A tangible way to use my position as a "senior" professor is to bring these voices together in mutual collaboration.

However, it becomes necessary to clarify that I, and all other authors, share our stories and significant contributions *beyond* our added value as Hispanic faculty members. We are scholars and faculty members who "made it" in Christian higher education because we are capable and worked extremely hard to overcome all obstacles. As Hispanics, we bring added value to our institutions and the academy, but our worth is not limited or even determined by our ethnic and cultural backgrounds. In both Christian higher institutions where I have served full time in the United States, many colleagues saw my primary value as a Hispanic professor, not as a significant professor and scholar.

For example, one of my colleagues at Southwestern was fired because he did not fulfill his sabbatical commitments. This situation was unusual, and the news shocked my department. We met to process what had happened to this colleague and to discuss the implications for our department. When we were together, the department chair's first comment was "You don't need to worry, Octavio. You are safe because you are Hispanic." At that moment, everything else did not matter but my cultural identity. At Talbot, our previous dean restructured some departments and programs and combined two departments. One of the programs they closed was related to our doctoral program. When my department was asked to meet with the dean to discuss these changes, all members wondered what implications they would have for us. As we were about to enter the dean's office, the senior member of our department turned to the other Hispanic professor and me and told us, "You don't need to worry, you are Hispanic, and you are safe." Again, at that moment, I realized that he saw our value primarily as Hispanics and not because of our academic achievements. In moments of crisis, the truth comes out.

Our journey as faculty members in Christian higher education institutions goes beyond the traditional one. It requires the ability to overcome obstacles as minorities and, at the same time, to always prove that we are not the token professors who received their positions without earning them. When I had just received my doctorate and was about to start teaching full time, the respected theological educator Elizabeth Conde-Frazier told me, "You need to work at least twice as hard as your colleagues to be respected." I have found her words to be true during my academic career.

My former professor and recognized Christian educator, Howard Hendricks, used to say in class, "You can do many things, but you need to make sure to find and do the things that you must do." In my case, being a professor and an academic leader represents my calling and vocation. The following sections about teaching, research, service, and mentoring continue sharing my journey in the professoriate.

Navigating Teaching

Teaching is only one of the four primary duties of faculty members, but it is the one that defines the professoriate. Most people equate being a faculty member with teaching and the workload with the number of hours teaching. After telling someone that I am a professor, I usually receive two questions: "What do you teach?" and "How many courses do you teach?" This common perception can be innocuous coming from people outside the academy but can bring negative consequences from the inside.

For example, when I was about to complete my doctorate and was exploring faculty positions, I had the opportunity to meet the president of Dallas Baptist University. A mutual friend arranged the unofficial job interview, hoping that this institution might be an ideal option for my future academic career because this president had direct influence over the hiring process. However, the first question he asked me after I told him I wanted to be a professor in a Christian higher education setting was "What do you want to teach?" My answer was that I was passionate about helping students learn and grow in the Lord. I had different interests in theological education, humanities, and the integration of faith and learning, but my primary calling was to be a professor regardless of the subject. My answer caught him by surprise and set the tone for a disastrous meeting that closed the doors of this institution for me. He assumed that I was confused and did not know what I wanted to do. He was expecting I would mention the specific courses I wanted to teach, but instead, I gave him a broader answer to reflect my calling. I obviously understood his question, but I wanted to express that my identity as a Christian professor was bigger than teaching a few specific courses. I earned academic degrees not to teach a few courses but to help others learn. As Christian professors, we teach people, not just content. At the end of our short meeting, the president gave me a personality inventory, encouraged me to reflect on my vocation, and told me to browse more through the university website. I never heard back from him, although we both attended the same church.

Nevertheless, the question remains relevant: "What do you teach?" I have taught multiple subjects in different countries and at different academic levels. I primarily teach doctoral-level courses in Christian higher education, foundations of education, and practical theology. Therefore, the answer to this question is complicated because it varies depending on the semester and setting. What remains consistent is that everything I teach has a biblical and theological foundation with practical implications. I consider myself a practical theologian because I believe that orthodoxy (correct belief or doctrine) and orthopraxis (proper practice) always go together. No one can really know God and not serve him, and no one can adequately serve God without knowing him.

My interest in the relationship between theology and practice started when I was fifteen with an event that shaped my life. My paternal grandmother died, and my uncle called for a family meeting. My uncle was a prominent Roman Catholic priest in Guadalajara and the self-imposed leader of the family. My parents grew up in traditional Catholic families and were the first and only ones to convert from Catholicism to Protestantism. They faced strong opposition from their families, friends, and society in general, to the point that my dad was fired from his job as an accountant in the Archdiocese of Guadalajara because he was a Protestant. This family meeting was the last time my father's family gathered together, and my uncle used that time to complain about his siblings. He told my dad that he had brought disgrace to his family because he had abandoned Roman Catholicism and became Protestant. My dad responded that he did not change religions but that he had found Christ and tried to explain with the Bible the reason for his new faith in Christ. My uncle stopped him and told him that all Protestants were ignorant and knew nothing about Christianity. He said that he, as a priest, had studied philosophy, theology, history, and other vital subjects, but Protestants only claimed to read the Bible without any formal training. My dad did not respond to his brother, but as I watched that conversation at a distance, I decided that if my faith in Christ was genuine, I needed to understand and defend it. This event spurred me to pursue theological training, understand how our faith or theology connects to our daily lives, and teach others. Teaching and theology are indeed practical and change people's lives.

Spanish is my heart language. Speaking English represents a great asset that allows me to teach in the United States and serve students worldwide. Being bilingual opens the door to different worldviews and contexts but also brings some challenges. I was born and raised in México, but now I am also a US citizen who lives with the tension of having two nationalities, languages, and cultural dynamics. The most challenging of all of them is, by far, the need to teach and speak with the highest academic standards in a second language. I find comfort in that Antonio del Corro, one of the most prominent Spanish Reformers and one of my faith heroes, also faced similar circumstances. Del Corro fled Spain persecuted by the Spanish Inquisition and ended up living in England after a complicated journey in different countries. He was a professor who spoke different languages but could not return to Spain. He wrote the following words:

> In the meantime, that of the place was not for me the least of my afflictions as a change of language. For being able to express in any way in the Spanish language the sensations of my soul, I am too often obliged to hesitate, to stammer in the language of Rome, and to betray my childhood. But nevertheless, since my unpolished speech is not unpleasant for you who value more what is said than with what flourishes it is

inflamed, I am neither jaded nor ashamed of the function entrusted to me. (translation mine)[3]

Teaching involves others. Teachers and students are mutually dependent on each other. I am a Hispanic teacher whose students constantly shape me as I shape them. I start all my classes with a *Calvin and Hobbes* cartoon. This practice allows me to create an informal shared meaning with my students through the years. Some of them have told me that they can no longer read *Calvin and Hobbes* without imagining a Hispanic accent in their minds. For most of my seminary students, I am the first Hispanic professor they encounter. In my case, the experience of teaching cross-culturally every day has made me a better person, looking forward to every teaching encounter to learn from my students.

Navigating Research

My greatest strength as a researcher is sometimes perceived as my greatest weakness. I love interdisciplinary work and have many diverse research interests. For this reason, I am a learner constantly seeking ways to discover new knowledge from others and collaborate with them. However, the higher education world, especially in the West, tends to value specialization and narrow research interests closely related to academic degrees. Most of my colleagues only attend conferences pertaining to their discipline, but I try to participate in different conferences beyond my particular areas of study. My strength is my ability to engage in different topics and conversations, but this diversity often might be perceived as a lack of specialization or depth.

Two examples illustrate my academic struggle as a "generalist" in a world of specialization. I like philosophy and have taught philosophy of education for many years, but I do not have an academic degree in philosophy. Years ago, I attempted to pursue a master's in philosophy during my first sabbatical, but I could not do it because my undergraduate degree was in literature. I tried to convince the program director that I knew the foundational background of this discipline and that I was looking forward to deepening that knowledge with their program. However, the assumption was that I was ignorant and could not understand their discussions because I lacked formal training in philosophy.

Similarly, as a practical theologian, I constantly seek opportunities to unite theology and ministry. However, I have found it hard to be a bridge between the disciplines of theology and practical ministries because faculty members in those areas tend to stay only in their academic lanes. I have experienced that Bible and theology scholars tend to look down on practitioners, especially educators. In the early stages of my career, I thought earning a doctorate in theology or Bible would grant me more academic respect and facilitate my desire for interdisciplinary work. However, I participated in a Wabash Center workshop for early career faculty members, where I met two colleagues with doctorates in theology who taught practical ministry courses in their institutions. They told me they faced similar circumstances of biblical scholars and theologians dismissing their opinions because their academic focus was on practical ministries, regardless of their academic degrees. After that experience, I decided to be at peace with my academic interests and continue pursuing a research agenda as a generalist and practical theologian in Christian higher education.

Hispanic scholars in Christian higher education must learn how to navigate the waters of predominantly White institutions, academic guilds, and settings. All minorities face similar circumstances where their minority status usually precedes their academic qualifications in the eyes of the majority group. I have experienced this situation my whole career, but it became evident in 2017 when I participated in several academic conferences in different spaces. The Spanish Reformation became one of my primary research interests, since I had the privilege of learning about it in 2010 when I spent one semester in Spain as a visiting scholar at the University of Seville. In 2017, it was the five-hundredth anniversary of the Reformation's beginning, and many institutions and groups organized conferences about this topic. I spoke about the Spanish Reformation in diverse contexts, but what remained a constant experience was that when I introduced myself to different scholars, they almost always asked me if Biola University or Talbot School of Theology had programs in Spanish where I taught. When I answered that I was a Christian higher education professor and I teach in English, they all looked surprised, they did not know how to respond, and most of them quietly moved away from me. They assumed that as a Hispanic scholar, my only area of expertise was Spanish. I understand that this unconscious bias resulted from a lack of representation in their academic experience and was not necessarily personal against me. Still, these situations contribute to the "racial battle fatigue" minorities face daily, which is also represented in the academy.[4]

Finally, as a bilingual Hispanic scholar with dual citizenship who ministers in both languages and cultures, I have found publishing in academic contexts designed for a single audience challenging. I live in the in-between spaces of the academy and the church, the United States and Latin America, and English and Spanish, and the academic world and publishers frequently lack structure and sensitivity to understand scholars like me. The publishing world is designed for monolingual and monocultural writers. For this reason, I have to write proposals and work with editors and publishers with different interests and backgrounds. It has been challenging to find agreement in a compartmentalized academic world.

Navigating Service

Service to the institution and society constitutes an essential academic duty. Faculty involvement in shared governance, committee work, and representing the institution to the broader community are central activities of the professoriate. In Christian higher education, service to the church adds a vital but extra responsibility to faculty members. All Christian professors should be involved in serving the Body of Christ, but this task becomes an expected responsibility for professors directly involved in theological education.

As a Hispanic professor, my service responsibilities seem similar to the ones of other faculty members. I attend faculty meetings, serve on committees, attend institutional functions, and serve in my local congregation. However, I constantly continue serving more than professors from the majority culture. For example, my institution awards promotion points for teaching, research, and service activities and requires a minimum number of points to grant the requested promotion. During my last promotion application, I realized that I had three times the required total points only in the area of service. My service to the institution, society, and church exceeded three times the points that professors need in all three areas combined!

Two reasons provide an explanation for these extra service activities. The first one is my holistic cultural perspective of life and ministry. I find it hard, if not impossible, to compartmentalize my different duties as a professor and my life outside the academy. Being a faculty member is not just my job but a key component of my vocation as a follower of Christ. For this reason, my writing projects, speaking engagements, and professional activities are not limited to the academic world, but all of them are integral elements of my attempt to live a holistic life. Several years ago, a Hispanic New Testament scholar shared with me how his colleagues were more productive and famous because of their many publications. However, they spent most of their time writing in their offices with closed doors. In his case, he felt the need to be with people and serve the church, although this prevented him from receiving the same recognition as his colleagues. In a way, most Hispanic and minority professors share similar tensions during their academic careers.

The second reason for my extra service activities, especially on campus, is my reality as a Hispanic professor in a predominantly White institution. This situation is not particular to Christian institutions but a reality of higher education in the United States. An article in the *Chronicle of Higher Education* called it "The Invisible Labor of Minority Professors."[5] All minorities become informal mentors, counselors, and advisors for other minorities. At the same time, they also become coveted representatives of minorities in committees and institutional task forces. In my twenty years as a full-time professor in Christian higher education, I have attended hundreds of meetings regarding the Hispanic community, ideas about how to attract more Hispanic students, and the possibilities of developing Hispanic programs. I also have been an integral part of institutional diversity and inclusion initiatives partly because of mutual interest and the need for community and in part because there is always a need for a Hispanic male voice on campus. This reality leads minority professors to do extra work without recognition, which sometimes prevents them from pursuing other academic opportunities that the institution values for promotion. This invisible faculty labor to the institution that becomes extremely time-consuming and frequently without recognition represents a foundational aspect that institutions must consider when attempting to reach the Hispanic community. It is impossible to become a Hispanic "Serving" Institution without the support and appreciation of Hispanic faculty members. Minorities perform many extra duties that nonminorities will never do without the appropriate compensation.

Navigating Mentoring

I clearly remember the words that Howard Hendricks frequently said in class: "You can impress people at a distance, but you can only impact them up close." Mentoring is, therefore, the professoriate's most transformative task. Nobody disputes the importance of mentoring in Christian higher education and the assumption that professors are indeed mentors to their students. However, mentoring tends to be the less-rewarded activity in the academy. Teaching, research, and service represent the three foundational expectations of higher education faculty members. The emphasis on these areas varies depending on the institutional culture. There are research- and teaching-oriented institutions, all of which require various levels of service. Mentoring is an expected duty and yet one that gets diluted among many other activities because professors, most of the time, do not receive promotional or economic incentives.

Promotion at my institution only focuses on teaching, research, and service. In my case, however, mentoring is central to my roles as dissertation advisor and director of doctoral research programs. In our doctoral programs, we use the expression "Doctors of the Church" to emphasize the communal aspect of our role as academic leaders.

Mentoring requires intentionality but also happens organically. A few years ago, I taught an undergraduate course at Biola University, where I encountered one of my best experiences as a faculty member. One of the students approached me after class with an unusual request that moved me to tears and reminded me of the immense influence I have as a Hispanic professor. This student was born in México but moved with her sister to the United States as a child after their parents passed away. She had an assignment for another class in which she was supposed to interview one of her parents about her family history. Neither the professor who gave her that assignment nor I had knowledge of her family situation. She told me that since I was born in México like her parents, I was the closest model she had to a father, and she asked me if she could interview me to complete the assignment. This experience made me more aware of how important my role is as a professor who teaches even without words and who mentors others at all times.

Conclusion

I remember my first commencement ceremony as a new full-time faculty member in Christian higher education. I was overwhelmed by the realization that I had the privilege of sitting next to senior and respected professors. I was sincerely grateful that I, a young Hispanic, received the opportunity to be a seminary professor. I constantly remind myself that God's grace is what gives me the honor of representing Christ to shape the minds and hearts of others. In the same way, I appreciate the increasing desire of predominantly White institutions to reach and serve Hispanics. I perceive a genuine interest in Christian higher education institutions to develop Hispanic programs and initiatives.

Nevertheless, after twenty years as a professor in these institutions, I also perceive the constant trend to keep Hispanics and Hispanic initiatives as token opportunities. True diversity—whether in institutions, churches, denominations, or any organization—is not about numbers or percentages but about inclusion in senior leadership, power in decision-making, and the ability to raise concerns and set the agenda. The alarming lack of representation in senior leadership indicates that Hispanics and minorities are helpful only if they submit or, even worse, assimilate into the dominant group and culture.

I now have earned the highest academic rank in my institution, and I am grateful. But I cannot fail to notice that many others from the dominant culture who are younger, with less experience, and without my formal training have been promoted to senior leadership positions. I applied to two critical positions without being seriously considered or receiving feedback from the search committees. At one faculty meeting with one of the final candidates, one faculty member asked why the final candidate was chosen over the others. One committee member answered that it was "because all other candidates were just awful." This unprofessional comment was particularly hurtful because I was sitting across the room, and we were colleagues in the same department. Nobody from the committee said anything in response to that comment or provided any clarification. The colleague who made that comment apologized to me after I brought it up a few days later. He told me he was joking with the final candidate because of his personal relationship. I know this situation was not necessarily personal against me. Still, it represents an inner-circle culture that lacks awareness of others who are forced to remain on the margins and simultaneously benefits those considered insiders. This is not a personal complaint but an example of the current reality in Christian higher education and most Christian organizations in the United States.

Another instance of the inconsistency between institutions' public support of Hispanic initiatives and the lack of support for Hispanic faculty members is the disparity in compensation for teaching courses in English versus Spanish. Theological institutions tend to develop programs in Spanish with similar, if not the same, English curricula, but many pay at least 30 percent less to professors teaching those courses. As a bilingual professor, I can teach in both English and Spanish. Still, instead of being compensated more for this important skill, I receive less money for teaching in Spanish without the consideration that the course has the same quality. The institutional justification for this situation is that students pay less for taking courses in Spanish, but the reality is that this disparity in faculty compensation tends to apply only to Hispanic professors. In this way, on the surface, institutions publicly announce their commitment to Hispanics, but in reality, Hispanic professors and programs receive second-class treatment and value.

Hispanic professors in Christian higher education serve "on the margins" in their institutions. This situation produces loneliness and also creates opportunities to shine as examples and role models to Hispanic students. A few months ago, I received a visit from two college students who unexpectedly showed up at my office. One of them saw the sign in Spanish on my office door, "Bienvenidos amigos" (Welcome friends), and my favorite soccer team logo, and he immediately felt seen. He brought his friend to meet me. They told me that I was the first Hispanic faculty member in theological education they had encountered. They said that seeing me as a professor and director of doctoral research programs gave them hope and expanded their imagination to pursue graduate studies and become professional leaders. This experience reminded me of how important my presence and ministry are as a Hispanic professor. Indeed, as one of my friends and colleagues frequently says, I have the best job in the world.

Notes

1 Parker Palmer, *The Courage to Teach: Exploring the Inner Landscape of a Teacher's Life* (San Francisco: Jossey-Bass, 2007), 1; Robert W. Pazmiño, "Teaching Both Who and Whose We Are: Honoring Individuality and Connection," *Christian Education Journal* 11, no. 2 (2014): 421–28.

2 Robert W. Pazmiño and Octavio J. Esqueda, *Anointed Teaching: Partnership with the Holy Spirit* (Salem, OR: Publicaciones Kerigma, 2019), 158–61.

3 Antonio del Corro, *Comentario dialogado a la epístola a los Romanos* (Seville: Editorial MAD, 2010), 99. For more information about Antonio del Corro and the Spanish Reformation, see Octavio Javier Esqueda, "The Spanish Reformation and Christian Teaching: Timeless Educational Principles from Antonio del Corro and Constantino Ponce de la Fuente," *Christian Education Journal* 11, no. 2 (2014): 336–49.

4 Jeremy Franklin, "Racial Microaggressions, Racial Battle Fatigue, and Racism-Related Stress in Higher Education," *Journal of Student Affairs at New York University* 12, no. 1 (2016): 44–55.

5 Audrey Williams June, "The Invisible Labor of Minority Professors," *Chronicle of Higher Education*, November 13, 2015.

2

MY EXPERIENCE AS A NON-WHITE, LATINA SINGLE MOTHER IN THE ACADEMY

Leticia I. Espinoza

My graduate training came as I attended public, secular institutions. So when I came to work at a small conservative evangelical university, I thought that the environment would be positive. The good news, if that's what we should call it, is that slow change is taking place at my home institution.

These years have been exhausting because my life experience is vastly different from those of the majority of my colleagues. I am not the embodiment of the expectations that so many have for a professor. I still do not feel "at home"; I do not know all the faculty on campus—almost half of them are new. I am out of place walking around campus. In truth, I now accept that I will never truly belong; I will never be the ideal type of "scholar that creates knowledge." For many, I will most likely never be more than the "Spanish teacher."

My Path to the Professoriate

The academic year of 2022–23 was my eighth year at a predominantly White, Christian institution. I am the only non-White Latina faculty member, a reality congruent with current research reporting that only 3 percent of all faculty in higher education are females of Latin American descent.[1] I am the only assistant professor of Spanish and oversee the program, although I am not officially the director or coordinator. Given the university's size, the Humanities Division houses Spanish alongside linguistics, philosophy, English, and history. This arrangement has benefits and detriments; for instance, the resources and knowledge my colleagues share have helped me refine my classes. On the other hand, being the only Spanish professor limits possibilities for traveling abroad or coauthoring articles, books, or even classes.

I reflect with gratitude for my access to some unique opportunities. Nevertheless, I recognize that only a few immigrants have the same access. I successfully achieved three academic degrees, but not because of exceptionalism or meritocracy. My road to the professoriate was not linear; I came to the United States to teach language and literature in higher education while finishing an engineering degree I started three years before arriving here. Since it was hard to work while I went to school in a small city in western México, my mother suggested I move to the United States with her, her husband, and my younger sister. I quickly realized how ill-prepared I was to survive in the culture. My lack of language skills and cultural understanding was the first hurdle. Besides my inexperience, my immediate family's understanding of the United States' mainstream culture, especially the educational system, was nonexistent. My mother and younger sister had been in the country for less than a decade before I arrived. Since my mother depended on my teenage sister to communicate with the English-speaking majority, her information on higher education was minimal. So I started taking English classes and was eager to be proficient enough to be admitted into a university. Alongside my classes, I worked in places that required me to speak the language. These jobs helped tremendously because now I had to communicate as the culture did. Finally, two years later, Calvin College (now Calvin University) accepted me in their engineering program and transferred some of my engineering credits.

I include these experiences in my path to the professoriate because it was not a straight line to finish one degree, let alone three. Instead, I see my experiences align with the three attributes Rosario Ceballo presents in her study "From Barrios to Yale: The Role of Parenting Strategies."[2] She notes that most successful Latinx students at Yale look back on their heritage with pride, have a relentless drive to excel, and believe in themselves.

Moreover, most of my extended paternal family are medical professionals who believed in the importance of education and greatly influenced me. Even though my parents did not attend high school, my mother also believed that some level of education was beneficial. My extended paternal family never questioned my bachelor's degree capability. Their questions instead focused on what practical and financially sound major I wanted to choose. They expected me to support myself and contribute to the Kingdom of God. Also, when I immigrated, I did not have the same financial burden or traditional gender roles other firstborn Latinas do.[3] I worked, but my mother did not expect me to sustain the family alone, although she relied on me and mostly my sister to function within the system.

Regarding my acculturation in the United States, perhaps it could be explained by the fact that I am a voluntary minority,[4] and I perceived institutions as opportunities because I had not experienced racism before emigrating.[5] In my country of origin, México, I am a majority, and while sexism is very much alive, racial prejudice does not restrict me. Here in the United States, I am first colored. More specifically, I am delimited as a Brown immigrant single mother—much is written on my body. Both historical realities and social misconceptions coexist and define who I am supposed to be in certain circles. As Kristie A. Ford explains, "Identities are not only shaped by self-perception but are influenced by others' perceptions of self as well. More pointedly, one's physicality or bodily self can be perceived differently depending upon the viewer."[6]

When I arrived in the United States, I was a Mexican woman, and now I am a Brown immigrant that happens to be a woman. How people relate to me outside the classroom and inside is greatly shaped by the perception of my phenotypical markers first, then my gender and immigrant status.

Navigating Teaching

As a predominantly White institution,[7] my home institution exhibits some of the same issues as other public and private institutions with similar demographics. For instance, tokenization and cultural taxation[8]; how these concepts present themselves is precisely in the perceptions of my hiring to support students of color, specifically Latinos, as opposed to the truth. At the time of my hiring, I was an ABD at Western Michigan University's

PhD program, and I am a native speaker of Spanish with awarded teaching and research experience. After the assistantship at Western Michigan University ended, I needed a job—primarily because, at the same time, I unwillingly became a single mom. While teaching at WMU equipped me to be in the classroom, nothing prepared me for life in academia in a predominantly White evangelical institution.

My current life as a professor parallels my experience as an undergraduate in an institution with a similar demographical makeup as the one I work for now. My intelligence and my right to attend the institution are constantly under scrutiny. Microaggressions and poor support systems are commonplace, making the environment isolating.[9] My experiences as a student followed my experience as a professor. This fact is not unique; Latinas must excel in a rather hostile environment that constantly questions their credentials and gaslights their negative experiences.[10] I am grateful for my position—I work on a beautiful campus and have made solid friendships with a few coworkers and alums. Also, I have been able to travel as part of my position, but I long for equity and justice in many areas. As a voluntary minority, I did not know how to deal with racism as a student, and it was challenging and even debilitating.[11] At the time, I did not have the language to describe my experience.

However, I can see how even my recent experiences align with ample research done on the physiological effects of overt and covert racism. Even today, I can feel my nervous system overact whenever I experience microaggressions at work. For instance, people assume that White males on campus hold a PhD, and some do not correct students when the title is wrongly applied. On the other hand, I have struggled for students to call me Dr. Espinoza and have even heard students excitedly talk about White male professors who ask students to call them by their first name. Learners deem the White male professor genuine, and the professor is oblivious to how this first-name basis undermines female and non-White professors. Then in evaluations, some of my courses have been labeled "dumb," and my time flexibility is "disorganized." Now hoping students will understand my perspective when I change a due date to benefit the class, I must explain how the United States is linear-time oriented as a low-context culture, as opposed to high-context cultures—which is the case for Latin America—that work with flexible time.[12] Medina and Luna explain, "Race and gender inequalities continue to permeate higher education institutions, for the culture and ideology of academe do not allow for differences. Academe is a model based on commonalities—not a community built around the concept of diversity."[13]

Previously, my assistantship at Western Michigan University required me to teach different levels of Spanish to a diverse student body. I had a variety of ethnicities in my classes—although White students were still the majority—different ages, majors, religions, and so on, which pushed me to exercise Christian hospitality in a way I had not done before. I appreciated the balance I had between research and teaching; when I got tired or frustrated with reading and writing term papers or my dissertation, I could prepare for class and grade (the only time grading seemed like a respite). It was an insulated position because I did not have to deal with any of the politics or department intricacies my professors did. Nevertheless, this experience marked how I relate to students and manage my classroom. I distinctly recall students reaching out to me. For instance, a single mom with little support asked if she could bring her child to a test; then the veterans with PTSD or the doctoral candidate that needed a 200-level course to complete their language requirement as part of a PhD program. Then the many LGBTQ+ students who timidly felt compelled to share their stories, the student who grew up in the foster care system, and the many heritage speakers were still very present in my mind. Teaching such a diverse classroom challenged me to discomfort, confused me at times, and required me to ask how I should minister to my students in a public institution.

I naïvely believed teaching at a Christian institution would be effortless; I already knew how to teach in myriad challenging situations, which led me to believe working with White Christian students would be easy, since we shared many values. I immediately learned I had to prove my expertise and my right to be their professor. Ford explains this phenomenon as the institution's normalization of characteristics and social groups that align with White hegemony (privilege, male-centered, heteronormative). Students come in with this worldview that assumes the correct knowledge repositories are White and male: "WOC [Women of Color] faculty, alien bodies within the academy, thus come to physically, behaviorally, and intellectually represent a raced and gendered 'other.' Disrupting the hegemonic classroom space, the presence of WOC faculty challenges White students' constructed understandings of effective pedagogical practices, curricular topics of importance, and outstanding scholarship. Female faculty of color are challenging the hegemonic worldview (e.g., Latino/as are lazy, African Americans are intellectually inferior, Asians are passive) in raced and gendered ways and they also have authority over student learning in the classroom."[14] I recall confronting one upper-level class after a few weeks into the semester when I noticed their veiled resistance to my presence in the classroom. In contrast to the intermediate-level class that seemed willing to accept my expertise, the upper-level students seemed uneasy and skeptical. I asked them, "Have you ever had a Latina professor?" Most of them shook their head negatively, except for one student of Latino heritage from Colorado. Then I added, "Well, I have never had all White students, so we are in this together." This outburst did not change anything as I had hoped. Nevertheless, I began to see how my very presence affected the classroom. To this day, it is as if my very presence is an act of resistance on campus.

I thought about how I would help my students understand that choosing to speak another language is more than just words. As Michael Pasquale and Nathan Bierma explain, "Language learning is more than just grammar learning. It is a decision to join a community of speakers."[15] Therefore, I focused on developing a framework for the classroom to guide students in engaging with a foreign language and the communities that speak it within the United States and abroad. At that time, the university had the Virtue Project as part of an agenda to help students develop character and academic prowess. Hospitality was one of the virtues, and it gave me a good starting point to explain how to participate in and outside of class. The following is what I have written on each of my syllabi:

> During this course, students will analyze different points of view, cultural mores, and perspectives. How to engage is an important topic for which to think and prepare. To fruitfully engage your worldview as you navigate this course, consider what Dr. Pasquale mentions in his book *Every Tribe and Tongue*: "language learning is more than just grammar learning, it is a decision to join a community of speakers." So, then, how should students thoughtfully and coherently engage as Christians? The following verses may also help: first, Matthew 22:39 (NIV): "Love your neighbor as yourself"

(the Gospels of Luke and Mark also share this story). Second, Leviticus 19:34 (NIV): "The foreigner residing among you must be treated as your native-born. Love them as yourself, for you were foreigners in Egypt. I am the LORD your God." As students, it will be essential to consider integrating faith in the different assignments.

As I mentioned, students still write severe evaluations, and I cannot eliminate the passive-aggressive attitudes that permeate the classes and do not allow for open disagreements. Nonetheless, I see much growth in several students regarding recognizing the Latinx community. Alumni work in Latinx-serving institutions in the city and abroad; many are teachers, social workers, and businesspeople in nonprofit and for-profit organizations. It has been a long and arduous road, but I feel hopeful and proud of how far my students and I have come as a community. I will continue to have students who feel uncomfortable with my presence. I will continue to challenge students' preconceptions. Nevertheless, I hope those willing to grow and learn in my classes will do so even after they leave my classroom.

Navigating Research

When I started graduate school, I immensely enjoyed the essays I had to write for my classes, more so than the exams. Teaching was a welcome respite from my classes, but I always looked forward to the final projects because I could expand and learn more about the topics that interested me. I hoped that this trend would continue once I started working in a higher education institution, but not so.

Given that time and energy are limited, the past administration suggested that I collaborate with other colleagues during a yearly review. This idea proved more difficult than expected. I am a single mother and a Latina immigrant, grew up Catholic, and am the only Spanish full-time professor. My research on Pan-Hispanic novelists explores questions that many of my colleagues never consider, questions of sexuality, gender, and national identity. The existing mainstream political conservatism looks at these topics with apprehension, concern, and even suspicion. Granted, not everyone thinks the same, but there is a subtle expectation to agree with the conservative majority.

I do not believe their intention is to sideline me, yet I feel a lack of trust, and then I doubt my ability and academic acumen. I constantly ask if there is something about how I conduct myself or present my ideas that gives the impression that I am not up to par intellectually.[16] I seldom talk about this. After all, I feel guilty because I do not want to be accused of ungratefulness or complaining; I constantly ask myself if I am exaggerating or misinterpreting.

Xaé Alicia Reyes and Diana I. Ríos validate my experience as they tell their journey as Latina women in higher education, explaining that "[they] hope to give voice to a silenced discourse that is often concealed for fear of appearing weak, confrontational, self-pitying, or unscholarly or for fear of numerous other labels that restrain Latina academics and others from discussing issues that need to be examined."[17] The implicit view that I may not be up to what is considered a scholar is ubiquitously in the air. The institution, like any other hegemonic White organization, operates under certain assumptions, ideals, privileges, and expectations that I do not seem to embody.

Ernest L. Boyer explains that higher learning institutions ought to grow and evolve into places where knowledge is shared among professors and practitioners for the common good, since scholarship is communal. He sees academic work as vital to the health of the nation, and he explains, "I'm convinced that in the century ahead, higher education in this country has an urgent obligation to become more vigorously engaged in the issues of our day, just as the land grant colleges helped farmers and technicians a century ago."[18] Boyer proposes a different paradigm of research, where "scholarship of engagement" is where the university's resources cover the needs of a community.

In this spirit, I applied for two grants in partnership with social sciences and then nursing and intercultural communications professors. For the first grant, the Inclusion Innovation Collaborative Grant, I worked with Dr. Nola Carew, director of social work and chair of the social sciences. We developed a series of events to encourage interaction among students and unaccompanied minor refugees based on Gordon Allport's Intergroup Contact Theory. We wanted our students to learn actively from different groups and exercise hospitality. To better equip students, Dr. Carew and I included the expertise of other professors and professionals to help students understand the history and current situation of the youth with whom they were to intermingle. We made the project part of one of the classes' requirements. At the end of the semester, students did a presentation where they included reflections and connections between the class's materials and their experiences with the youth. For the second grant, the Faith in the Vaccine Grant, I recruited Latinx alums to do outreach and bring COVID-19 information and resources to the Hispanic communities in the city and around. I also planned events for faculty, staff, and students alongside Dr. Maria McCormick, the director of nursing, and Dr. Eunice Hong, professor of intercultural studies. At the end of these projects, I strengthened relations within the community with colleagues and students.

Furthermore, many of my courses have required me to research and apply the acquired knowledge more practically. For instance, I have classes where students must develop interactions with the Hispanic communities in the city. They must learn about businesses, churches, and other supporting institutions. Then they must contact a member of these organizations and interview them to connect people's real lives with the materials from class. My classes and the grants have allowed me to emphasize the importance of recognizing Latinos, and other minority groups, as the image of God, fully human and not people that need to be saved but instead served and included as a vital part of the socioeconomic well-being of the city. I am not a traditional researcher for many reasons (and to top it all, I like comics, which has been another point of discord with some colleagues), but I pursue a scholarship of engagement. My students acquire knowledge in my classes, but we also serve our community and create relationships.

Navigating Mentoring

A significant part of my job is advising students who need help planning their classes for the next two to five years. Most of my advisees have declared Spanish as a major or a minor, but I also talk to anyone who wants to learn about the program and what it would mean for their vocations. Furthermore, only some of my students or advisees become mentees. I have great relationships with alums I mentor, even if I was not their academic advisor.

In my journey, Latino alums in different careers have reached out and built relationships with me. In the same way, I seek to support Latinos who have never had me as a professor.

When I started at my home institution, I served as a faculty mentor for a student group, Ritmos, which initially focused on Spanish learners, and Latinos were welcome too. Since the attention centered on Spanish students, the first leadership group included an intelligent group of female students, but then the shift to serve Latinos and invite Spanish learners occurred not so subtly. A space to connect and form a community needed to be created.

So Latinx students born abroad and in the United States, who now make up 7 percent of the student body, are meeting regularly for fellowship. This point is crucial because, according to Tara Yosso et al., extracurricular activities are essential for the well-being of students:

> Often social counter spaces develop out of academic ones, and vice versa. Social counter spaces allow room outside the classroom confines for students to vent frustrations and cultivate friendships with people who share many of their experiences. Primarily student-initiated and student-run, social counter-spaces exist on and around campus, through both formal and informal activities (e.g., dinner gatherings, community outreach programs, campus cultural centers, intramural sports, cultural floors in residence halls, and ethnic newspapers or radio shows). Building community in social counter spaces cultivates students' sense of home and family, which bolsters their sense of belonging and nurtures their resilience.[19]

Our campus climate struggles to be welcoming for non-White students. In the spring of 2021, we—a Latino alumnus who worked in admissions, a professor of social work who was the chair of the diversity committee, and myself—conducted a focus group with around fifteen Latinx students. No formal meeting minutes and no action plan resulted, but from the notes collected, I can confidently say that students feel reduced to simple stereotypes. Statements such as "I will never want to be rooming with a Mexican again," "This is what I got back for living with a Mexican," and "One time I was cooking some Mexican food, and my roommate was asking a lot of questions: 'What is that? That is so weird, we never put that kind of stuff in my food'" show prejudice without any inclination to a hospitable curiosity that creates a safe space for conversation, not without uncomfortableness, but safe and respectful.

Moreover, their language is not seen as prestigious or essential, and many times it is used against them: "When we talk in our language, we receive looks, you know," or when a student is addressed in childlike sentences in Spanish: "I felt like Dora; it wasn't really me." Latinx students feel overlooked, and professors must be educated about the many differences among the Hispanic populations to be better equipped to tackle racial questions that may arise and recognize their blind spots and biases.

Students also talked about support structures like mentors, chapels in Spanish, Latinx host families, and community outreach, to name a few. We, the organizers, extended our sympathies and support, and hope that the university will support students, not force them to abandon their identities.

Navigating Service/Administration

In the summer of 2020, my home institution changed its administration. As a result, many in faculty leadership have left, and their years of collective knowledge will not be easily replaced. In addition, the university is enrollment-dependent, and the administration is focusing on overhauling the current divisions to create schools hoping to streamline redundancies and reduce overhead.

The implications of these changes are also disquieting; new faculty have been hired, and they have good experience and education, but they have deep knowledge of how to do things in their new institution, which makes the void much clearer to see. The question of who has which responsibilities is ever-present, as is the news of people leaving or trying to leave. Such confusion can be unsettling and discouraging, especially as I am close to my pre-tenure-track interview. Also, students have felt the vacuum left by the transitions, particularly international students whose visas and working hours must be consistently monitored.

As I approach my pre-tenure review, I have conducted research and secured grants. Regarding service, as part of my portfolio, I served on the diversity committee for over three years, the online courses committee for one year, a special Higher Learning Commission committee, and various hiring committees. As mentioned above, these committees can become overwhelming. Another female professor of color candidly mentioned that as a minority, she got invited to many meetings, and then she laughed about this situation. She was able to make light of the situation while pressing how non-White faculty are tokenized and taxed culturally.

Today, there are more opportunities for persons of color in the academy, and no one pursues this calling in Christian higher education to make a name for themselves. We want to see students succeed, and we want to live sustainable and healthy lives. As a non-White, Latina single mom who came to the United States as an immigrant, I've faced significant challenges. And I'm still learning what it means to be a scholar. Many women of color have experienced similar frustrations and joys as they have charted their careers. My hope is that in sharing my story, more schools will consider carefully how they can embrace and create more hospitable environments for their Latinx students and faculty. There is still much work to do.

Notes

1 "Fast Facts: Race/Ethnicity of College Faculty," US Department of Education, Institute for Educational Sciences, National Center for Education Statistics, May 2022, https://nces.ed.gov/fastfacts/display.asp?id=61.

2 Rosario Ceballo, "From Barrios to Yale: The Role of Parenting Strategies," *Hispanic Journal of Behavioral Sciences* 26, no. 2 (May 2004): 173.

3 Ceballo, 180.

4 John Uzo Ogbu and Herbert D. Simons explain that a voluntary minority emigrates willingly for any reason. Their relationship to institutions is vastly different from those of involuntary minorities due to colonization, conquest, or slavery. For a complete overview, please see John Uzo Ogbu and Herbert D. Simons, "Voluntary and Involuntary Minorities: A Cultural-Ecological Theory of School Performance with Some Implications for Education," *Anthropology and Education Quarterly* 29, no. 2 (June 1998): 164–66, https://www.jstor.org/stable/3196181.

5 Kristie A. Ford, "Race, Gender, and Bodily (Mis)Recognitions: Women of Color Faculty Experiences with White Students in the College Classroom," *Journal of Higher Education* 82, no. 4 (2011): 444.

6 Ford, 444.

7   It is 76.33 percent White according to collegefactual.com. This information is not readily available on the university's website.

8   Ford, "Race, Gender, and Bodily (Mis)Recognitions," 445.

9   For more on microaggressions, see Tara J. Yosso, William A. Smith, and Daniel G. Solórzano, "Critical Race Theory, Racial Microaggressions, and Campus Racial Climate for Latina/o Undergraduates," *Harvard Educational Review* 79, no. 4 (2009): 661–62.

10 Catherine Medina and Gaye Luna, "Narratives from Latina Professors in Higher Education," *Anthropology and Education Quarterly* 31, no. 1 (March 2000): 48.

11 One current resource is Robert T. Carter and Alex L. Pieterse, *Measuring the Effects of Racism: Guidelines for the Assessment and Treatment of Race-Based Traumatic Stress Injury* (New York: Columbia University Press, 2020), 45–46.

12 To explain this topic, among other cultural differences in class, I use Erin Meyer's book *The Culture Map: Breaking through the Invisible Boundaries of Global Business* (New York: Public Affairs, 2014).

13 Medina and Luna, "Narratives from Latina Professors," 48–49.

14 Ford, "Race, Gender, and Bodily (Mis)Recognitions," 447.

15 Michael D. Pasquale and Nathan L. Bierma, *Every Tribe and Tongue: A Biblical Vision for Language in Society* (Eugene, OR: Pickwick, 2011), 41.

16 Medina and Luna, "Narratives from Latina Professors," 49.

17 Xaé Alicia Reyes and Diana I. Ríos, "Dialoguing the Latina Experience in Higher Education," *Journal of Hispanic Higher Education* 4, no. 4 (October 2005): 378.

18 Ernest L. Boyer, "The Scholarship of Engagement," *Bulletin of the American Academy of Arts and Sciences* 49, no. 7 (April 1996): 28.

19 Yosso, Smith, and Solórzano, "Critical Race Theory," 677.

3

LITERATURE AS ABSOLUTE NECESSITY

Michael Jimenez

Narrative is more than communication; it is also history.

—Mario T. García

That reading is writing, taking notes is writing, watching film is writing, copying is writing.

—Kate Zambreno

Reflection should be easy for a historian. My job is interpreting the past. However, personal memories seem so subjective. My first instinct is to hide behind citations—others speaking in my place. I find safety in striving to be objective and neutral when talking about others, which was the method I was taught, but I cannot help listening to my inner voice whispering to me that objectivity and neutrality are illusions. However, I am still striving.

Decades ago, books changed my life. Life before books appears foggy in my memory, almost dreamlike. I make time for books at hours of the day when I would not for a living, breathing person. It is important to me, vital really. In terms of my own life, it has an event-like nature. There is no going back to life before books. It would be a betrayal of *the* event.

History provides paths, roads taken and not. There are moments preserved by memories that provide literature for us to learn about the past.

Some of this literature receives more attention than others, as do only some memories. Part of my own evolving path to my present roles revolves around, you guessed it, books. Some of my earliest memories are of my father taking the family to the bookstore. For instance, one of the first books I received was a beautifully illustrated *Robinson Crusoe* by Daniel Defoe, a childhood favorite of my father. Years later, I would return to one of these bookstores located in downtown Long Beach called Acres of Books, which is unfortunately no longer in existence. I loaded up on cheap, used paperback philosophy, theology, and fiction books. These books led to more and more books filling my shelves until I had so many that some found their way into the outside shed because I ran out of space, but I kept buying new ones.

Navigating books as a reader, as a student, and finally, as a teacher shaped the person I am. My love of reading allowed me to be a professor. Therefore, when I reflect on my role as a teacher, researcher, and mentor, the only way I can be faithful to myself remains in my relationship with books.

I can honestly say that my love of books led to my life in academia. My journey is not the typical route. I took a few community college classes here and there but ended up working full time in the aerospace field. Suddenly, like a Damascus Road experience, I started reading theology books from my dad's personal library because I was listening to preachers and theologians on the radio and online. I grew up in a Christian home and attended a Christian school all my life, so reading a bit of Luther and Bonhoeffer was not a struggle. They spoke a familiar language. In fact, when I began attending my father's Spanish-speaking church around the same time, my tentative link to the Spanish language was my biblical knowledge.

I must have looked odd to my coworkers: quickly consuming my sandwich at lunch, almost unconsciously, because Luther's commentary on Galatians engrossed me. However, reading Dostoevsky's *Crime and Punishment* catapulted me back to community college full time. One of my coworkers, Philip Song, recommended this novel to me, since he saw I liked to read so much. I acknowledge my debt to the Russian novelist with his bust on my office bookshelf. I can still recall reading his novels, normal time stopping.

All I cared about at that moment was the book's universe. I would read with a dictionary and journal nearby so I could learn words I did not know. The old dictionary and the journal serve as testimonies of my dedication to literature. Learning to read this way also taught me the importance of solitude. Then and there, I realized I wanted to be a professor.

The interdisciplinary nature of my teaching and research was formed at a community college. I voraciously read anything that interested me. My curiosity and openness to learning about the world were fostered from the beginning of my academic journey. However, as a first-generation Latino student, it was uncharted territory.

Poet and essayist Cynthia Cruz explains similar experiences to mine growing up in the United States with a Latino immigrant parent: "I grew up with a basic belief in character. My father told me repeatedly, and modeled for me, the basic tenet that the suffering we experience forms us, creating character, and that character—not wealth, popularity, or power—is what matters in this life."[1] I can almost hear my father's voice reading Cruz's lessons on character. I heard about *caracter* over and over from him. Again like Cruz, I attended community college in my twenties; furthermore, as a child of mixed parentage, I had a challenging time fitting in with my classmates. Life was a constant struggle with belonging. On the one hand, I am not Latino enough because I am not fluent in Spanish, and on the other hand, I am not White enough simply because of my last name. As Cruz states: "Nor am I 'just' American."[2] It would take me years to confront this ambiguous identity through my writing, but it was always in the back of my mind.

My first big break, presenting the possibility that going back to college to become a professor was not an absolutely insane idea, came from a Saturday-morning English course taught by Dr. Joy Zhao in the spring of 2002. I was already a voracious reader, but the fact that Dr. Zhao published three of my student essays, including one entitled "A Supervisor's Dream to Become a Professor," in her textbook of students' writing revealed to me that I was now a writer. More opportunities to publish my writing would materialize while I studied in grad school, but Dr. Zhao's grace boosted my confidence. I would need to be an optimist because it took years to settle into a full-time job in academia.

At some point, I stopped writing *this* essay and read over my recent articles and essays. They are more autobiographical, featuring my father, who is from Costa Rica. I did not want *this* piece to be a repetition of these recent essays. I even went back and read that "Dream" essay in Dr. Zhao's book. A couple of things surprised me about that piece. First, I was obsessed with talking about books, even in the "Dream" essay. Second, I realized that the "Dream" essay is almost completely silent about any facet of my Latino heritage. There is one reference to me dreaming of finally traveling with my family to visit my extended family in Costa Rica, which I finally got to do in real life a few times. This piece is definitely a dream because I also saw myself living in a nice place along Malibu's shores based on my teaching salary alone! I started my journey in academia and my personal life in 2002, not fully realizing the long road ahead in about another decade of college, culminating in the search for a full-time position for about the following decade. Stopping to review my journey helped me consider something that the Norwegian author Karl Ove Knausgaard said: "Writing is about making something accessible, allowing something to reveal itself."[3] These very early essays like the "Dream" one are immature and trivial, but I am grateful they exist to help reveal the journey in my own words for the next twenty years.

The hustle of getting a teaching job in academia was exhausting, physically and mentally. What fascinates me is that Cruz's own experience, what one of my favorite writers, Kate Zambreno, calls "the amazing traveling adjunct" about her own experience, remains one of the few accounts that sounds like mine.[4] It is rare to read about the adjunct's plight from writers like Cruz and Zambreno in such brutal transparency. How can two published authors of many books be in such distress? Where does that leave me? Teaching somewhere between six and ten classes a semester while writing and researching without health insurance is stressful. For instance, the only way my wife's two pregnancies were anything resembling affordable was because of my aerospace job's health insurance (yes, I kept my aerospace job while also adjunct teaching and working in a doctoral program). There were moments over the last decade wondering if my identity would always be "the amazing traveling adjunct." Reading Cruz and Zambreno reminded me of those days of driving between campuses and sleeping in the car before a three-hour evening class. Nothing paints a better picture of the adjunct hustle than having a ready-made Caesar salad from the gas station for dinner and falling asleep in the adjunct office before the evening class, hoping the snoring was not too loud.

I realize for all my struggles as a working student and then an adjunct that I was extremely fortunate. I did most of this while still living with my parents, who gave me a stable home life—stability to the point of boredom. But boredom is just another way to say that I did not have some of the worries that so many others experience. A life framed by two predictable parents meant a life missing dramatic chaos. I remained in California, since I did not want to uproot my family for *my* dream job.

One of the best opportunities I received was teaching world civilizations classes at the beginning of my doctoral program. It was also one of the scariest and most uncertain moments. It was scary because I had never taught a class before, and it was uncertain because how was I supposed to teach about *world* history? I consulted my notes from my undergraduate years to help craft my lectures.

As a student, I loved a good lecture. However, it seems that the lecture has fallen on hard times. It has been labeled old-fashioned; the students are too passive in the classroom. However, Mary Cappello declares, "Midway between a sermon and a bedtime story, the lecture is knowledge's dramatic form. Nonfiction's lost performative: the lecture."[5]

What is frightening about lecturing for a world history class is that there is no bottom when it comes to knowledge of the subject. There is always going to be something left out. Moreover, specialization will prepare the instructor to be knowledgeable about potentially one narrow subject. Preparing for these lectures is what exposed my own blind spots in global knowledge. This idea was clear to me when I noticed the gaps in my notes—where were all the notes from Asian, African, and Latin American history, any area not in the United States, Germany, France, and England?

Approaching students as a monolithic blob does not do justice to their creative potentiality. As Cappello writes, "Fastened to our seats in the lecture hall, we aren't funnel-heads into which a lecturer's knowledge is poured. We are haunted beings trailed by past trials, we are shadows of our barely realized truths, evidence of our existence, bathed in the light, or dark, of future wanderings."[6] The students and the lecturer are all haunted beings with past experiences, yet we all can have something new revealed to us.

The most exciting and rewarding part of being a historian is the research. I can spend hours lost in a bookstore or library, searching the pages for new information about myself or the outside world. I agree with Cruz when she declares, "Entering the world of the book is always so much more fulfilling than entering the world itself."[7] Good books give good companionship.

If we care about the communicative properties of literature, then like a good friendship, we will not shy away from listening to a book when it tells us the uncomfortable truths about ourselves. One truth is that a quick scan over history reveals that so many voices were denied a literary audience. Even in my lecture notes, there was an incomplete picture. There is no "voice of the voiceless"—the voices are there in many books; the point is to read them. In fact, we do not spend enough time applauding the role of translators and how they have made available so many wonderful books. Translated books leave us little excuse for worldly ignorance, especially for us educators. If I am asked why I like to research so much outside of my specialization, I might respond, "Because of the thrill of surprise." The research I have in mind is not just reading a few textbooks, the equivalency of a Wikipedia page, trying to quickly cover blind spots in our knowledge. It is the joy of discovery, like when you meet a new friend.

Global literature complicates a simplistic view of history. Historian Teofilo F. Ruiz points out what a clear-eyed study of history teaches us: "The terror of history is all around us, gnawing endlessly at our sense of, and desire for, order. It undermines, most of all, our hopes."[8] When I was an undergraduate at Biola University, Dr. Judith Rood mentored me on this point. First, she was able to expound on her family history, including the horror of the Holocaust, and connect it to her theological commitments, culminating in her own stunning surprise of converting to Christianity. Second, she illuminated the world of Middle Eastern history and literature, which helped make my understanding of Christianity grounded in that ancient historical world. My relationship with Dr. Rood formed the balance between theology and history. I learned to have a profound respect for literature outside of my comfort zone, and instead of shying away from it, I wanted to take baby steps in waiting for what it was revealing about the world and myself.

The willingness to not hide from the terror of history remains an important ideal in my research and teaching. However, I do not think this is something to consider lightly. For example, in his book *Brown Church*, writer Robert Chao Romero presents Latino/a students struggling with their faith, considering some of the terrible violence in the past committed by the church.[9] When there only seem to be either/or options, then we will continue to see the abandonment of the church and the academy, especially by Latino/a students.

Romero's students' existential crisis resonated with me. Here is someone like me with a deep commitment to Christianity not willing to discard it at the first sign of trouble, who does not then mercilessly attack it with the same zealous vigor that they once had defending the faith, but honest enough to see that terror of historical moments with the church playing the role of the antagonist. Romero serves Christian educators and church leaders by illustrating a crisis of conscience so many Latino/a students are being forced to struggle with over identity and faith. How do we then answer the terror of history problem?

One of the only ways I can think of an answer is with books, since that is what I am trained to do. I agree with the Peruvian novelist Mario Vargas Llosa and his statement about how good books serve as bridges across time and space: "Literature creates a fraternity within human diversity and eclipses the frontiers erected among men and women by ignorance, ideologies, religions, languages, and stupidity."[10] We live in a moment where more literature is translated and accessible than ever in human history. There is no excuse not to begin reading these *other* voices.

The impulse to diversify our syllabus may be at a new high in academia, and it is an important step toward making our lectures and writings mirror reality. However, there remains the danger of trying not to be so Eurocentric that you unconsciously quote others for their "exotic" impact.[11] There is a danger of showing how many non-Europeans you can quote to impress that you are truly up to date with the latest academic trends of the twenty-first century; the so-called Western canon and classics be damned. I have wrestled a lot with checking my Europhilia, but much European literature remains an interest, a focused part of my studies, and what I like to read for pleasure. For example, my doctoral thesis was on Swiss theologian Karl Barth and the Enlightenment, and at the tail end of my research, I became interested in theories about modernity outside of Europe. Since I became more interested in theory from Latin America and the Islamic world, I started exploring this literature. No one taught me to diversify my syllabus. It is something that happened almost accidentally. I started reading one book, following up with essays, interviews, or podcasts with the author. If the original book interested me, I wanted to learn more about the writer. This formula usually ended up leading to more books by the author or some of the books they enjoyed. This formula became a way to build a bridge of books across the literary world, integrating Vargas Llosa's idea of the fraternity of literature the best I could.

Pointing out the problems of Eurocentrism does not mean excluding the reading of European classics. For example, writer Nathalie Etoke argues that "knowledge must be decolonized and school curricula diversified," but even she still has her "invisible community of Europeans" that she continues to read.[12] To read only one's niche is to reenact the same errors of previous generations. Imagine, for instance, if one day I decided I would only read and cite writers from Central America. That will almost exclude every author I cited in *this* essay. This mindset betrays the fraternity of literature and its accessibility. However, Etoke reminds us of a valuable lesson about how this fraternity is often managed: "Lies by omission abound in history books."[13]

For instance, one of the reasons I recently chose to research Cesar Chavez was I grew frustrated at seeing books about Christian peacemaking where Latino/as are still omitted. The same omission applies to Central American history and literature. If it were not for my Costa Rican cousin giving me her books when I visited Costa Rica a couple of years ago, I would have little access to the literature of my dad's country of origin. The tide is changing, but we must beware of assuming a book labeled Latino/a means it directly appeals to all Latino/as. Latin America has a varied history, including its literature. Perhaps because of my father's roots, I did spend a year reading nothing but Central American literature; that does not mean this method should apply universally. However, historically speaking, we should recognize what literature is often missing in this fraternity of books and look for ways to include them in both the classroom and our home libraries.

My commitment to academia is to come prepared to class by research-ing the class materials and introducing students to writings that inform, inspire, and sometimes irritate. Maybe I am lucky, but I rarely have dealt personally with the competitive side of academia. In fact, Latino/a academ-ics especially showed me the greatest hospitality, mentoring me through a friendly chat over coffee while I was in traveling-adjunct limbo.

My father once told me, "You are Latino. Do not let anyone take that from you." The reactions I receive from people, including Latino/as, about who I am make me doubt this sentiment. From being called an "under-cover Latino" to customer service staring at my driver's license and back to my pale-yet-reddish face, my last name yields some funny responses. Even recently, while getting a haircut, the hairstylist was amazed by my last name. My usual deadpan response is "Yes, you guessed it. My dad is from Costa Rica."

The Latino/a academics I have met over the years have been encourag-ing, especially since my research has turned toward Latin America for about ten years now. But apart from the scholarly conversations, they have helped point out that one might experience some microaggressions because they are Latino or other actions that are simple oversights, but that can be irritating. For instance, I might be an "undercover Latino," but I have been mistaken a couple of times for that *other* Latino professor in the department.

The frequency of Spanish in the house came when my grandma and uncles started arriving in the United States, so learning Spanish was always a game of catching up. Years later, I eventually realized that attending a Spanish-speaking church did not automatically make one fluent in Span-ish. At my best, my speaking continues to be sloppy Spanglish that never knows where to place the *me, te,* or *se.* Furthermore, witnessing the birth of a Spanish ministry partnering with an English-speaking church, I got a first-row view of aggressions toward too many Latino/as in the church. I might call them little transgressions now, but in retrospect, being told dirty baptismal water is fine enough or the Spanish-speaking ministry vote does not count when voting on trivial matters like a new file cabinet appears hostile.

One example continues to bother me from a church I was attending. One evening, the senior pastor declared directly to the bilingual members of the congregation that they were only to attend the English-speaking service.

The Spanish ministry was only for monolingual Spanish speakers. He was emphatic on this point, to the point it made me feel very uncomfortable. This was the church that was partly responsible for motivating me to begin listening to theologians and ministers on my commute and reading theology books from my dad's library. This decision was taken away in a country that boasts the freedom of choice and preference. I was not privy to what power struggle was happening behind the scenes. It was one of the last services I attended before attending the church where my Spanish-speaking father preaches every Sunday. This was also about the same time I went back to community college, so many big shifts were happening in my life. Moments like these are formative for all the wrong reasons. Still, they do illuminate how much damage can be done when not respecting other cultures and languages, especially from a place of power and influence.

The above scenarios reveal that books are not going to solve everything; as Vargas Llosa said, stupidity is one of the artificial barriers preventing human growth, but I already was gaining enough self-awareness to leave that space. As a teacher and mentor of sorts, I want to follow the ideas suggested by Knausgaard that writing reveals something about ourselves and again from Vargas Llosa that there is a fraternity of literature waiting to be read. My own struggles with identity could possibly be like the same situation my students are experiencing. Similar but not the same.

A good example is the text I quoted early in the essay from Cynthia Cruz. We have some similar experiences as adjuncts and White Latino/as, yet there are also major differences, particularly in gender orientation. Places of familiarity really resonated with me, but that did not mean Cruz and I have the exact same experiences. This opening quote to an essay by the author Kali Fajardo-Anstine, which I have had many students read, describes the complexity of identity: "'What are you?' is a question I've been asked by strangers since I was a child. As a little girl, I didn't know how to answer this question with a simple one-word, one-identity response. And I still don't. I knew then just as I know now that we were many things. We were American, we were Mexican, we were Filipino and Spanish and Jewish."[14] Fajardo-Anstine continues the essay by going deep into the difficulty of researching the Indigenous roots of her identity. It was the discovery of an old recording of her grandmother that opened the world of archival research for her novel. This revelation uncovers the type of wonderful research that is ready to be exposed to someone searching out the meaning of their own identity that may be hidden away in the family closet. Helping students realize that they and their families have a history, one that is worth telling, remains one of my greatest pleasures as an instructor. As Fajardo-Anstine declares, "When the official archives ignored our existence, within the closets of our homes, our records were waiting, our stories powerfully alive."

I am proud of the Latino heritage I inherited from my father. Literature from US Latino/as and from Latin America are some of my favorites. However, the experience of being Latino/a is multifaceted. There is not one book that encompasses the experience. The most I can do is point to a selection of the great library over time and see if the student has an experience like I had when I read from Dostoevsky, Luther, or Cisneros. My struggles with my own identity were not solely answered within books. I gained much illumination from my Mexican American wife and family, my extended Costa Rican family, my church, and my students. Watching my two sons both experience their own growth about identity fascinates me, and I hope to mentor them in a way that allows them the freedom to explore it well.

Perhaps this is why I have always had difficulty becoming pigeonholed into just one discipline. At the heart of my research and writing has been storytelling. The role of the humanities makes the opportunity for good storytellers possible. A good writer is one who has the freedom to explore history but also the imagination. Historical fiction, for example, is not to be read as a history textbook, but because of its traces of history within the novel form, it is nonetheless a historical document. Thus, it is encouraging to see scholars like Chicano historian Mario García write a historiography book that details much of the writing that I have discussed in this essay. By bringing in narratives like novels, autobiographies, memoirs, and testimonios, he validates the idea that everyone's story is worth telling.[15] In this sense, García adds a historiographical foundation to Fajardo-Anstine's research of her family. Before the reader balks at the idea of learning about history from reading Chicano literature, for example, keep in mind the great omission of the Chicano/a experience from US history books. The same would apply to Central American or anything we might imagine as "minority" literature.

Writing allows the mundane and ordinary to find narration. My finest moments as a teacher remain viewing my students' research into family members' histories. To narrate everyday life and give these ordinary moments attention highlights the importance of literature, challenging the hierarchies of historical research that were absorbed with the comings and goings of powerful men.

Books still mean the world to me. I open each day in quiet solitude with a book before the whole neighborhood wakes up. Recently, when my wife and eldest son got COVID-19 and were isolated to another room, my youngest boy and I were in quarantine. Realizing I was imprisoned in the house for a week, I decided to read Min Jin Lee's *Pachinko*. I received the book as a Christmas gift a few years ago, but its daunting size and my busy schedule allowed me to keep the book on the shelf. Reading Lee's novel was like time traveling back over twenty years ago to the evenings I read Dostoevsky's *Crime and Punishment*. All I wanted to do was read Lee's book. I was upset if mundane moments like washing the dishes interfered with my reading. However, unlike that earlier memory, something unique happened: Lee's book made me weep twice actually. Perhaps there are books out there in bookstores or even sitting for years on your bookshelf that will change your life. You will never know if you do not pick a book up and read.

Notes

1 Cynthia Cruz, *The Melancholia of Class: A Manifesto for the Working Class* (New York: Repeater, 2021), 13.

2 Cynthia Cruz, *Disquieting: Essays on Silence* (Toronto: Bookhug, 2019), 18–19, 118–19.

3 Karl Ove Knausgaard, *Inadvertent*, trans. Ingvild Burkey (New Haven, CT: Yale University Press, 2018), 27.

4 Kate Zambreno, *Drifts: A Novel* (New York: Riverhead, 2020), 138; Cruz, *Melancholia of Class*, 6; Cruz, *Disquieting*, 19. Another writer who writes about the difficulty of motherhood, adjunct labor, and writing is Kate Zambreno. Like Zambreno, I was under so much stress teaching a large load of classes that I got shingles across my stomach and back.

5 Mary Cappello, *Lecture* (Oakland, CA: Transit, 2020), 13.

6 Cappello, 48.

7 Cruz, *Disquieting*, 154.

8 Teofilo F. Ruiz, *The Terror of History: On the Uncertainties of Life in Western Civilization* (Princeton, NJ: Princeton University Press, 2011), 9.

9 Robert Chao Romero, *The Brown Church: Five Centuries of Latino/a Social Justice, Theology, and Identity* (Downers Grove, IL: InterVarsity Press, 2020), 1–6.

10 Mario Vargas Llosa, *In Praise of Reading Fiction: The Nobel Lecture*, trans. Edith Grossman (New York: Farrar, Straus and Giroux, 2010), 9.

11 Gabriel Zaid, *The Secret of Fame: The Literary Encounter in an Age of Distraction*, trans. Natasha Wimmer (Philadelphia: Paul Dry Books, 2008), 26–32.

12 Nathalie Etoke, *Shades of Black*, trans. Gila Walker (New York: Seagull Books, 2021), 92.

13 Nathalie Etoke, *Melancholia Africana: The Indispensable Overcoming of the Black Condition*, trans. Bill Hamlett (New York: Rowman and Littlefield, 2019), 18.

14 Kali Fajardo-Anstine, "On Roots and Research: Accessing Who You Are and Where You Come From," *Gay Mag*, January 29, 2020, https://gay.medium.com/on-roots-and-research-b078ee3e3dc0.

15 Mario T. García, *Literature as History: Autobiography, Testimonio, and the Novel in the Chicano and Latino Experience* (Tucson: University of Arizona Press, 2016), 4, 170.

4

BUILDING *COMUNIDAD*

Succeeding in Academia as a
First-Generation Latina Professor

Itzel Meduri Soto

The minuscule percentages haunted me. I received an email from the provost informing me that I had obtained tenure at my institution. What should have been a moment of pure joy and excitement was overshadowed by an overwhelming sense of sadness and guilt. Confused, I called a friend as I attempted to process what I felt and why I felt that way. He graciously listened as I stumbled through words, at times intercepted by my tears. Latine professors comprise 4.6 percent of tenured faculty in the United States, and less than 2 percent of Latina women hold tenure.[1] I was part of the "select few," and I was supposed to feel exceptionally proud and accomplished, and I did, but I also felt undeserving. I was experiencing what some psychologists have called "success guilt." Success guilt is a common phenomenon among first-generation college students from marginalized backgrounds who feel guilty for standing out as academic achievers when many of their family and community members struggle to keep themselves alive. It sounds like a paradox, but I didn't feel undeserving because I felt I was less deserving than the 79 percent of White faculty who make up all tenured positions, but precisely because I knew that ALANA[2] faculty are just as deserving. Frankly, I resented the fact that I could be used as an example, albeit a bad one, that "proved" that systemic barriers that excluded people like me in higher education did not exist.

In 2015, when I obtained my doctoral degree, only 7 percent of all PhDs awarded that year were earned by Latine students.[3] In 2019, that number grew to 7.5 percent, but the difference between White and Latine groups remains abysmal—57.4 percent of all people who earned a PhD identified as non-Hispanic White.[4] The degree attainment of Latines decreased at every degree level in 2019:

Degree	Hispanic Share (%)	White Share (%)
Associate's	23.8	51.2
Bachelor's	14.2	59.1
Master's	9.5	53.7
Doctorate	7.5	57.4

Source: *Postsecondary National Policy Institute, 2021.*

At the faculty level, the numbers are even more sobering:

Faculty Level	Hispanic Share (%)	White Share (%)
Assistant	6	70
Associate	5	74
Professor	4	79

Source: *National Center for Education Statistics, 2020.*

There is parity between males and females in both ethnic groups, except at the professor level between White males (51 percent) and White females (28 percent). The lack of representation among Latine faculty continues even as the share of Latine college students more than doubled, from 9 percent to 20 percent, between 1997 and 2017. During this span, the share of Latine faculty had a modest increase from 3 percent to 5 percent. At least 70 percent of faculty at all levels, including contingent faculty, are White.[5] In 2007, 91.1 percent of faculty at Christian colleges and universities were White; in 2017, that number dropped to 79.34 percent.[6] However, the percentage of Latine faculty during that period only increased from 1.79 percent to 3.59 percent, while the percentage of Latine students at CCCU institutions grew from 5.27 percent to 10.62 percent.

Even at Hispanic-Serving Institutions (HSIs), Latine faculty are dearth. Not-for-profit higher education institutions that enroll at least 25 percent of full-time Latine undergraduate students are eligible to obtain HSI designation. At the national level, HSIs represent 20 percent of all colleges and universities but enroll more than 65 percent of all Latine collegegoers.[7] Yet faculty representation in these institutions still paints a grim picture. The Latine-student to Latine-faculty ratio at four-year HSIs is 146 to 1, compared with 10 to 1 for White students and faculty. Private institutions have one Latine faculty member for every 264 Latine students and one White faculty member for every eight White students.[8] As I reflect on these numbers, I am grief-stricken; but it is not a grief that paralyzes me but one that grounds me and propels me forward. In a study conducted about first-generation Latine students who experienced success guilt, academic success for these students was driven by their desire to support their family and community.[9] As a Latina Christian faculty member, I resonate with the motivators of these students.

Although studies show that the success of ALANA students and faculty depends on their connection to the community, "community building is almost antithetical to academia."[10] The stereotype of the lone old White man who sits at his desk for hours and inhabits, through his readings and writings, only the theoretical space and disconnects himself and his work from the "real world" has persisted in academia for far too long. Nevertheless, Jesus presents us with a different model of scholarship. Emulating Jesus means entering "the cultural, religious, and social reality of the people" even in our academic practices.[11] As I think about my own practices and seek to resist self-centered models, these questions help me remain grounded: How is my research benefiting the Kingdom of God? Does my research take into consideration the social realities of people? Am I accumulating knowledge simply for self-interest or to boost my ego? How can I continue learning from others—inside and outside academia? As a Christian scholar, I highly value community engagement, but academia has not traditionally fostered these types of opportunities. Traditional venues for disseminating research are limiting—academic papers and books tend to have a small readership, many conference presentations have low attendance rates, and for the most part, scholarly work operates in a vacuum. What are some alternative ways in which academics can remain relevant and continue their conversations with a broader audience, thus having a bigger impact in their communities? The use of social media platforms can, for example, help transcend some of the aforementioned limitations and connect faculty with an extensive network of people on a global scale. Partnering with churches and other organizations and writing for a popular audience can also generate opportunities for engaging with a wider audience. We do a disservice to ourselves and to others when we disregard nonacademics, who are the majority of individuals in the world.

Trabajo bruto pero con orgullo
Aquí se comparte, lo mío es tuyo
Este pueblo no se ahoga con marullos
Y si se derrumba, yo lo reconstruyo[12]

I am from Wilmington, California, a city in the Harbor area of Los Angeles County that is 90 percent Latine and 40 percent immigrant.[13] My city has more refineries than green spaces, and among news outlets, it is only recognized for its gang violence and high crime rate. The median household income is more than 50 percent below the state's average, and 93 percent of high school students are economically disadvantaged. Unsurprisingly, educational attainment is just another manifestation of the systemic injustices that plague my city; only 5.8 percent of residents ages twenty-five and older have a bachelor's degree[14] compared to the 37.9 percent of adults nationally of the same age group.[15] A brief overview of the demographics above would make some people question *Can anything good come out of Wilmington?*

The statistics won't reveal my mother's crucial role in my academic formation. Forty-two percent of people with PhDs have at least one parent with a master's degree or higher,[16] and tenure-track faculty are twenty-five times more likely than the general population to have a parent with a doctorate.[17] My mother didn't have social capital conferred to her through advanced degrees, a prestigious career, economic power, access to a network of influential people, or even a strong command of the English language, but her courage and determination were instrumental in my own educational advancement. My mother was a school teacher in her native Jalisco, México, before migrating to the United States in her twenties. As the second oldest among twelve siblings, she learned the meaning of hard work at an early age. At age five, she would accompany my grandfather at dawn to help him with agricultural work, and when she wasn't at school, she was helping take care of her eleven siblings.

When she became a teacher, she was sent to a small rural town where she was the "town's teacher." During those days, the townspeople believed that teachers had a wealth of knowledge and capabilities in different aspects of life, including the medical field. One day, my mother was asked to administer an injection to a sick, elderly woman. Contrary to the townspeople's expectations of what a schoolteacher should know how to do, my mother, the schoolteacher, did not know how to inject. However, admitting this would have made the townspeople question my mother's ability to be a good teacher. My mother did the only thing she could at that moment: pray to God and administer the injection hoping everything turned out favorably. By the grace of God, this woman recovered from her illness. And it was only by God's grace, because my mom did not realize she had to mix in the diluent with the medicine and only injected water into this woman. Through these experiences, my mother eventually did learn how to inject people (properly), and forty-five years later, she still helps people with their injections. My mother is a person of great courage and wit who raised me in a foreign country where people like her, a Brown woman with limited English proficiency who could not validate her teaching degree in the United States and became a factory worker, were assumed ignorant and incompetent.

My mother didn't only inspire me; she created opportunities for me in a place where she wasn't given many. When my teachers told her that she shouldn't speak to me in Spanish, unbeknown to them, she felt strongly encouraged to augment her supply of Mexican workbooks so I could continue practicing my Spanish literacy skills. When I became enamored by the book series *The Boxcar Children*, she would assess my comprehension by asking me to summarize the books to her—in Spanish, of course. Twelve-hour work shifts did not stop her, and her involvement in my school affairs took the shape of frequent notes to my teachers and daily check-ins with me. At age twenty-two, I became part of the 2 percent of teen moms earning a college degree by age thirty, having had my son at nineteen.[18] My mother did not waver in her support; she financed part of my college education and gifted me with hundreds of hours of childcare, always reminding me, *¡échale ganas!* (give it your all). Mi mami was my fiercest advocate in a system that projected my failure.

> *There is a nation*
> *I'm born and raised in*
> *It is supposed to be my home*
> *I am a stranger*
> *Here in my own land*
> *Everyone hears it in my tone*[19]

A Filipina-American student approached me after class following a discussion about the concept of familism, a cultural value in the Latine community that emphasizes the importance of family interconnectedness, commitment, and loyalty. She had been distraught by the fact that one of her professors had jokingly said that living with one's parents after age eighteen was a sign of immaturity and a flawed character. In Spanish class, we discussed how moving out of the parents' home before getting married was generally not considered a good thing and often indicated intrafamilial conflict. Students had also learned that Latine along with Black and Asian families are more likely than White families to live in multigenerational households and that this was a typical living arrangement in biblical times. My student, who had been made to feel ashamed by her professor because she still lived with her parents, expressed a sense of relief by obtaining a different lens on this issue, one that affirmed her family's living arrangement. The professor's comment pointed to a lack of cultural awareness that harmed this student's self-perception.

The *othering* that ALANA students are subjected to is not exclusively manifested through insensitive comments made by White professors. We all swim in the same poisonous waters of White supremacy. As a Latina woman, I have also had to unlearn behaviors and ways of thinking that dehumanize God's children. For example, as a Spanish major, there are gaps in my education that resulted from the blatant erasure of Black and Indigenous communities. I learned to exalt the voices of those with the most power and prestige in the Spanish-speaking world. I learned canons that ignored and misrepresented women, Black people, and Indigenous people. My educational background taught me to engage in linguistic discrimination against Latines who didn't speak Spanish or didn't speak it "properly"—I was made to feel ashamed of my abuela's *haigas* and *comistes*.[20] I've also had to reject sexist and racist notions embedded in my own cultural upbringing and develop an awareness of how my lighter skin affords me unmerited privilege in a society that upholds pigmentocracy because "we cannot belong to one another if we're not committed to telling the truth about ourselves and each other . . . so we must tell the truth about the past—and the ways we have disrupted our sacred belongingness—so that we may heal our future."[21] Healing is birthed from truth, and one must embrace a posture of humility in order to receive truth. As a teacher, God has entrusted me with the education of thousands of students, and I have an obligation to confront my biases and remain humble so that I can allow God's correction in my life and learn how to love in a manner that resembles that of Christ's more and more every day.

I admit that it is easy to be discouraged when one strongly believes that long-lasting transformation lies in rebuilding a whole system. However, as I reflect on Jesus's ministry, I am reminded that he challenged political systems, confronting Pharisees and Herodians alike and changing a system of condemnation to one that made a path for our salvation, *but* he also spent time tending to the disenfranchised and the stigmatized. I was in middle school when Mr. Mulkey called me smart and encouraged my mother to consider enrolling me in the gifted program at the high school I would soon attend. In high school, Mrs. Vargas applauded me for thinking critically instead of interpreting my vocal disagreements with aspects of the subject matter as disrespect. I was in college when Dr. Gómez approached me after class and asked me if I had ever thought of earning a doctorate. "Yes," I replied, pretending to know the meaning of *doctorate*. Then he volunteered to be my mentor under the McNair Scholars Program, a government initiative designed to increase the attainment of PhD degrees by historically excluded members of society. Dr. Gómez, a Spanish literature professor, taught me that *my* interpretation of the text mattered, that I could—and should—bring in my whole self to class because that would make me a better, more authentic thinker. He gave me, a young woman from Wilmington, California, the confidence to travel across the continent as an undergraduate to Seville, Spain, where I would present my research on Puerto Rican author Ana Lydia Vega's work. Dr. Gómez's mentorship and the mentorship I received as part of the McNair Scholars Program were vital in helping me succeed as a PhD graduate. I perceive my mentoring relationships as having been crucial in ensuring my academic success, and it is through this lens I approach mentoring now as a faculty member.

Students benefit from mentors who have a similar racial identity to them and shared lived experiences.[22] Although women and ALANAs are more likely to evaluate their mentoring relationships as "extremely important,"[23] research shows that ALANA students are less likely to be mentored than White students.[24] ALANA faculty have a stronger commitment to mentoring historically excluded students than their White peers,[25] but the lack of diversity within the professoriate hinders students' access to ALANA mentors. Mentoring ALANA students at predominantly White institutions (PWIs) is an undertaking that involves more than career coaching and academic advice. Students who find themselves in these spaces will often see their ALANA mentors as advocates with whom they can relate; the wisdom from the faculty's experiences becomes an invaluable asset in this relationship. In a study conducted on how mentors establish trust with ALANA students, it was determined that "listening, maintaining excellent communication, having a holistic understanding of the protégé, self-disclosing, using humor, being willing to discuss race and culture, acknowledging mistakes, and behaving with integrity" were integral components in promoting trust.[26]

One day, a mentee emailed me about her intention to drop out. She said that the university was requesting certain information that would force her to divulge her parents' undocumented status, and she did not feel safe releasing that information. She hadn't replied to the email, and feeling rattled, she planned to disappear from campus. A strong relationship with this student based on trust allowed her to confide in me a delicate matter that she perceived as a barrier to continuing her education. Upon learning of this situation, I immediately connected with people on campus whom I trusted, and together, we were able to help this student continue her education and eventually graduate.

Recently, I became aware that a Latina colleague in my department had been instrumental in helping an ALANA student be admitted into a graduate program. Her aid extended far beyond what is considered typical: She spent hours with the student sorting out her classes so she could graduate in a timely manner. She spoke with the student's parents about what this opportunity meant because the faculty member knew that the parents' support was crucial to the student in this process. She helped her navigate the financial implications of this decision. The student told me, "Dr. Hernández changed my life. I know God put her in my life for a reason." I also learned that this faculty had raised funds at her church so a Latina student struggling to pay tuition could finish her semester. Dr. Hernández knew how to best help these students because of her own experiences as a first-generation immigrant student. When I asked Dr. Hernández why she hadn't mentioned any of this in her promotion application, she replied, "Because the university does not recognize this type of mentorship as valuable."

Mentorship can help create a sense of belonging, and experiencing a sense of belonging is vital in ensuring the success of students and educators alike.[27] Facilitating an environment that creates a sense of belonging for ALANA faculty is not only the "good Christian" thing to do but also a wise business practice, especially considering that many ALANA faculty are leaving academe, citing feelings of isolation and exclusion.[28] Higher education institutions were built exclusively with the White male in mind, and predominantly White institutions are inherently individualistic; that is, single-authored papers are given more worth than multiple-authored articles, institutions often operate as ivory towers that are completely disconnected and disengaged from the surrounding local communities, staff and faculty are rarely given opportunities to intermingle, departments across campus tend to function in isolation from one another, and even the nomenclature of "schools" points to a firm separation. The individualistic character of PWIs contrasts with the values of ALANA faculty, who tend to value meaningful relationships with others.

> *Todo aquel que piense que está solo y que está mal*
> *Tiene que saber que no es así*
> *Que en la vida no hay nadie solo, siempre hay alguien*[29]

My family and Latine community taught me the importance of laboring collaboratively and never allowing yourself to be siloed because this will almost always guarantee self-destruction. I grew up on Lakme Avenue, surrounded by neighbors who were also my family members. We had an open door and fridge policy that allowed us to easily enter one another's homes and eat one another's food without trepidation. My mom had a strict rule regarding food: *Aquí la comida no se guarda ni se esconde* (Here, food will not be set apart or hidden). She thought that was *un acto muy feo*—a very bad act. It was on Lakme Avenue where I learned that God created us as interdependent beings in need of community—in need of *convivencia*. *La convivencia* is one of those words that does not have a translation in English that justly captures its meaning. People are said to be *conviviendo* if they are wholly present with each other in the moment, spending time together to enjoy each other's presence, with no ulterior motive in mind. People that engage in *convivencia* do so peacefully and respectfully in a manner that fully recognizes the humanity of everyone involved. Theologian Gary Riebe-Estrella says that "*vida* for Latinos is understood within our socio-centric cultural world as a shared reality . . . not simply *vivencia*, but *convivencia*. . . . As such, *convivencia* speaks of the intimacy out of which *la vida* comes."[30]

As a Latina faculty member, I desire those moments of *convivencia*. *Convivir* with people from my institution has become a lifeline that allows me to develop a sense of belonging in an environment that can be especially difficult for women and ALANAs. I seek and prioritize opportunities where I can spend time with people from different areas of the university with the intention of *convivir*. A few years ago, I joined an intramural soccer team at my university formed by faculty, staff, and students. I met people I would probably never have interacted with if it wasn't for this (unconventional) opportunity. This semester, I invited all the Latina faculty and staff I knew on campus (there are not many of us) to meet weekly to discuss a theology book written by a Latina author. We met at my house once a week for eight weeks and developed an intimate bond over meals, confessions, and reflections. Our weekly meetings became a "Xicana sacred space," a space that bred knowledge, strength, resistance, inspiration, and sisterhood.[31] A couple of years ago, I started having regular dinner gatherings with some colleagues at a local restaurant with the intention of *convivir*. This group of faculty represents people from different schools and diverse ethnic backgrounds who recognize the importance of equity work and are committed to justice issues. It is within these groups that I find a sense of belonging.

However, *la convivencia* isn't always as straightforward as one might assume. Notions of gender, particularly in faith-based institutions, play a role in who gets to *convivir* with whom and under which circumstances. Believing women are temptations that must be avoided turns cross-gender *convivencia* into a sinful act. Latina women, who tend to be exoticized and hypersexualized, become especially "dangerous" under this framework. I once "interrupted" a male space at a university luncheon by intentionally choosing to sit at a table occupied by only men. Apparently, I was wearing my invisible/hypervisible suit that day, because they ignored me *and* became tense with my presence. Men are overwhelmingly overrepresented in leadership roles across all academic landscapes, and this disparity is even more evident in CCCUs.[32] If men, who occupy most positions of power in the workplace, limit their access to women, they also limit women's access to opportunities. Instead, Aimee Byrd suggests that evangelicals depart from the temptation model and embrace one of *sibling solidarity*, where men and women value each other as kin, worthy of affection, harmony, and respect.[33]

The careers of female faculty are gravely affected by gendered ideologies, and ALANA women carry the double burden of sexism and racism, even within student-teacher relations. Studies show that female faculty are expected to be motherly, nurturing, and lenient in the classroom and are harshly criticized by students when they don't conform to these expectations.[34] In addition, students evaluate women and ALANA faculty more poorly than White men, which bears significant weight in a context where student evaluations are used to determine employment (i.e., contingent faculty), promotion, and tenure.[35] Students also show greater classroom incivility toward ALANAs and female faculty, especially when the subject they're teaching relates to gender and race relations.[36] The experiences of female ALANA faculty across the nation coincide with my own experiences in the classroom; I've received numerous grade appeals, many requests for extensions, and a sudden drop in my student evaluations after incorporating a social justice framework in my classes, and I have had unsettling confrontations with students. One student refused to exit my classroom after I asked him to leave due to his confrontational language, which made me feel unsafe. Still, the most traumatic experience I've had thus far occurred when a student confessed he thought about killing me. Of course, these events were psychologically disturbing but also very time-consuming and mentally taxing. As I shared my experiences with both male and female colleagues, it was evident that female faculty are particularly targeted. Experts often recommend inclusive teaching practices that assume that all teachers have the same conferred level of authority and disregard the gender and racial identity of the instructor.[37] Inclusive teaching practices that do not consider the instructor's identity can pose safety concerns and generate further inequities in the educational landscape. As we labor toward a more equitable educational setting, we must consider these factors.

> *Y me diste nombre*
> *Yo soy tu niña*
> *La niña de tus ojos*
> *Porque me amaste a mí*[38]

I grew up with the motto *aprovecha las oportunidades* (take advantage of opportunities) because people like us don't get many. It took me until six years into my career to realize that *aprovechar las oportunidades* doesn't always mean saying yes to every perceived opportunity I encounter. First, we must consider that not all "opportunities" are actually beneficial to our students or us; some are exploitative and work only to advance the university's self-interests, interests that oftentimes operate against our communities. For ALANA faculty, many of these "opportunities" may present themselves as diversity work. Still, a university that is not genuinely committed to equity and inclusivity will have us running around on a hamster wheel, feeling exhausted and defeated.

Other times, it is necessary to say no to *aprovechar* moments of sacred rest, the type that fills you, not because of what you're *doing* but because of *who you are*. An old deceiver called *impostor syndrome* approached me and said, "You are not enough. You're lucky you're here. Be grateful that you're occupying a space that doesn't belong to you, and work incessantly, desperately trying to prove your worth. And whatever you do, don't disrupt the status quo," and God replied, *"Mija, vales oro. Usa tu voz,* and don't ever become so comfortable in this space that you turn a blind eye to the injustices around you." So I will use my voice even when I'm trembling because I know my Creator.

Notes

1 "Fast Facts: Race/Ethnicity of College Faculty," US Department of Education, Institute for Educational Sciences, National Center for Education Statistics, May 2022, https://nces.ed.gov/fastfacts/display.asp?id=61.

2 ALANA stands for African, Latine, Asian, and Native American. The term was developed by Donald Brown at Boston College.

3 "Doctorate Recipients from U.S. Universities: 2015," Science and Engineering Doctorates, National Science Foundation, https://www.nsf.gov/statistics/2017/nsf17306.

4 "Latino Student Fact Sheet: September 2022," Postsecondary National Policy Institute, https://pnpi.org/wp-content/uploads/2021/08/PNPI_LatinoStudentsFactsheet_July2021.pdf.

5 Leslie Davis and Richard Fry, "College Faculty Have Become More Racially and Ethnically Diverse, but Remain Far Less So Than Students," Pew Research Center, July 31, 2019, https://www.pewresearch.org/fact-tank/2019/07/31/us-college-faculty-student-diversity/.

6 Council for Christian Colleges and Universities, "Diversity Matters: Race, Ethnicity, and Christian Higher Education," *Advance*, Spring 2020, https://www.cccu.org/wp-content/uploads/2020/04/Spring-2020-Advance-low-res.pdf.

7 "A California Briefing on 25 Years of HSIs," Excelencia in Education, March 2, 2021, https://www.edexcelencia.org/.

8 Nicholas Vargas, Julio Villa-Palomino, and Erika Davis, "Latinx Faculty Representation and Resource Allocation at Hispanic Serving Institutions," *Race Ethnicity and Education* 23, no. 1 (2019): 39–54, https://doi.org/10.1080/13613324.2019.1679749.

9 Rosean Moreno, "The Guilt of Success: Looking at Latino First-Generation College Students' Experience of Leaving Home," *Journal of Hispanic Higher Education* 20, no. 2 (2019): 213–31, https://doi.org/10.1177/1538192719849756.

10 Lorgia García Peña, *Community as Rebellion: A Syllabus for Surviving Academia as a Woman of Color* (Chicago: Haymarket Books, 2022), 25.

11 Ana María Pineda, "Pastoral de conjunto," in *Mestizo Christianity: Theology from the Latino Perspective*, ed. Arturo J. Banuelas (Eugene, OR: Wipf & Stock, 2004), 126–31.

12 Calle 13, "Latinoamérica," track 7 on *Entren los que quieran*, Sony, 2011, compact disc; Daniel Calveti, "La niña de mis ojos," track 6 on *Anclado a tus promesas*, Gracia Producciones, 2020, accessed October 12, 2022, https://open.spotify.com/track/6MFIKcaEXhXhTieiNbmr0P?autoplay=true.

13 "Race and Ethnicity in Wilmington, Los Angeles, California (Neighborhood)," Demographic Statistical Atlas of the United States—Statistical Atlas, accessed November 1, 2022, https://statisticalatlas.com/neighborhood/California/Los-Angeles/Wilmington/Race-and-Ethnicity.

14 "Phineas Banning Senior High School in Wilmington, CA—Best High School U.S. News and World Report," US News, accessed November 2, 2022, https://www .usnews.com/education/best-high-schools/california/districts/los-angeles-unified -school-district/phineas-banning-senior-high-school-2515. See also US Census Bureau, "American Community Survey (ACS)," accessed November 3, 2022, https:// data.census.gov/table?q=DP02&g=860XX00US90744.

15 US Census Bureau, "Census Bureau Releases New Educational Attainment Data," accessed October 13, 2022, https://www.census.gov/newsroom/press-releases/2022/ educational-attainment.html.

16 "Doctorate Recipients from U.S. Universities: 2016," Science and Engineering Doctorates, National Science Foundation, Arlington, VA, https://nsf.gov/statistics/ 2018/nsf18304/.

17 Laura Spitalniak, "Tenure-Track Faculty Are Likely to Have Parents Who Went to Grad School—a Trend That Hasn't Changed for 50 Years," Higher Ed Dive, August 31, 2022.

18 Saul D. Hoffman, "By the Numbers: The Public Costs of Teen Childbearing," National Campaign to Prevent Teen Pregnancy, 2006.

19 Micah Bournes and Lucee Bournes, "Water," JOT Track Productions, 2020, single, 3:58.

20 These are linguistic variations that are widely used by Mexican people but are considered "incorrect" by linguistic purists.

21 Kat Armas, *Abuelita Faith: What Women on the Margins Teach Us about Wisdom, Persistence, and Strength* (Grand Rapids, MI: Brazos, 2021), 72.

22 Rowena Ortiz-Walters and Lucy L. Gilson, "Mentoring in Academia: An Examination of the Experiences of Protégés of Color," *Journal of Vocational Behavior* 67, no. 3 (2005): 459–75, https://doi.org/10.1016/j.jvb.2004.09.004; Stacy Blake-Beard, Melissa L. Bayne, Faye J. Crosby, and Carol B. Muller, "Matching by Race and Gender in Mentoring Relationships: Keeping Our Eyes on the Prize," *Journal of Social Issues* 67, no. 3 (2011): 622–43, https://doi.org/10.1111/j.1540-4560.2011 .01717.x.

23 "Study: Women and Minorities Value Mentoring Programs, but Findings Reveal Opportunities for Improved Effectiveness," Heidrick & Struggles, Chicago, December 17, 2017, accessed November 11, 2022, https://heidrick.mediaroom.com/2017 -12-27-Study-Women-and-Minorities-Value-Mentoring-Programs-But-Findings -Reveal-Opportunities-for-Improved-Effectiveness.

24 Kecia M. Thomas, Leigh A. Willis, and Jimmy Davis, "Mentoring Minority Graduate Students: Issues and Strategies for Institutions, Faculty, and Students," *Equal Opportunities International* 26, no. 3 (2007): 178–92, https://doi.org/10.1108/ 02610150710735471; W. Brad Johnson, *On Being a Mentor: A Guide for Higher Education Faculty* (New York: Routledge, 2016).

25 Kimberly A. Griffin, "Voices of the 'Othermothers': Reconsidering Black Professors' Relationships with Black Students as a Form of Social Exchange," *Journal of*

Negro Education 82, no. 2 (2013): 169, https://doi.org/10.7709/jnegroeducation.82 .2.0169; Kimberly A. Griffin, "Institutional Barriers, Strategies, and Benefits to Increasing the Representation of Women and Men of Color in the Professoriate," *Higher Education: Handbook of Theory and Research* (2020): 277–349, https://doi.org/ 10.1007/978-3-030-31365-4_4.

26 Anne Chan, "Trust-Building in the Mentoring of Students of Color," *Mentoring & Tutoring: Partnership in Learning* 26, no. 1 (2018): 4–29, https://doi.org/10.1080/ 13611267.2017.1416265.

27 Keonya Booker, "Connection and Commitment: How Sense of Belonging and Classroom Community Influence Degree Persistence for African American Under-graduate Women," *International Journal of Teaching and Learning in Higher Education* 28, no. 2 (2016): 218–29; DeLeon L. Gray, Brooke Harris-Thomas, Joanna N. Ali, Taylor N. Cummings, Tamika L. McElveen, and Tamecia R. Jones, "Urban Middle Schoolers' Opportunities to Belong Predict Fluctuations in Their Engage-ment across the School Day," *Urban Education* (2022), https://doi.org/10.1177/ 00420859221117682; Meena M. Balgopal et al., "A Sense of Belonging: The Role of Higher Education in Retaining Quality STEM Teachers," *PLOS ONE* 17, no. 8 (2022), https://doi.org/10.1371/journal.pone.0272552.

28 Joshua Doležal, "Why Faculty of Color Are Leaving Academe," *Chronicle of Higher Education*, September 22, 2022.

29 Celia Cruz, "Mi vida es un carnaval," track 9 on *Mi vida es cantar*, RMM Records, 1998, compact disc.

30 Gary Riebe-Estrella, "Theological Education as Convivencia," in *From the Heart of Our People: Latino/a Explorations in Catholic Systematic Theology*, ed. Orlando O. Espin and Miguel H. Díaz (Maryknoll, NY: Orbis, 1999), 211–12.

31 Lourdes Diaz Soto, Claudia Cervantes-Soon, Elizabeth Villarreal, and Emmet Campos, "The Xicana Sacred Space: A Communal Circle of Compromiso for Educational Researchers," *Harvard Educational Review* 79, no. 4 (2009): 755–76, https://doi.org/10.17763/haer.79.4.4k3x387k74754q18.

32 See Karen A. Longman and Patricia S. Anderson, "Women in Leadership: The Future of Christian Higher Education," *Christian Higher Education* 15, nos. 1–2 (2016): 24–37, https://doi.org/10.1080/15563759.2016.1107339.

33 See Aimee Byrd, *Why Can't We Be Friends? Avoidance Is Not Purity* (Phillipsburg, NJ: P&R Publishing, 2018).

34 See Kristie A. Ford, "Race, Gender, and Bodily (Mis)Recognitions: Women of Color Faculty Experiences with White Students in the College Classroom," *Journal of Higher Education* 82, no. 4 (2011): 444–78, https://doi.org/10.1353/jhe.2011 .0026; Chavella T. Pittman, "Race and Gender Oppression in the Classroom: The Experiences of Women Faculty of Color with White Male Students," *Teaching Sociology* 38, no. 3 (2010): 183–96, https://doi.org/10.1177/0092055x10370120.

35 Bethany Fleck and Aaron S. Richmond, "Does the Instructors Gender Identity and Syllabus Design Affect Students Perceptions of Their Instructor?," *Teaching of*

Psychology (2022), https://doi.org/10.1177/00986283211072742. See also Lillian MacNell, Adam Driscoll, and Andrea N. Hunt, "What's in a Name: Exposing Gender Bias in Student Ratings of Teaching," *Innovative Higher Education* 40, no. 4 (2014): 291–303, https://doi.org/10.1007/s10755-014-9313-4; Landon D. Reid, "The Role of Perceived Race and Gender in the Evaluation of College Teaching on Ratemyprofessors.com," *Journal of Diversity in Higher Education* 3, no. 3 (2010): 137–52, https://doi.org/10.1037/a0019865.

36   Diana B. Kardia and Mary C. Wright, "Instructor Identity: The Impact of Gender and Race on Faculty Experiences with Teaching," *University of Michigan Center for Research on Learning and Teaching Occasional Papers*, no. 19 (2004).

37   Chavella Pittman and Thomas J. Tobin, "Advice: Academe Has a Lot to Learn about How Inclusive Teaching Affects Instructors," *Chronicle of Higher Education*, July 14, 2022.

38   Daniel Calveti, "La niña de mis ojos," track 6 on *Anclado a tus promesas*, Gracia Producciones, 2020.

5

SEARCHING FOR HEALTH

A Latino's Academic Journey

NATHAN L. CARTAGENA

Who I am, where I am coming from, and where I wish to go shape the method and content of my theological work.

—Ada María Isasi-Díaz[1]

We, all Puerto Ricans, are colonial subjects; refusing to name that existential condition . . . is to mask the insidious colonial architecture that undergirds a racist and imperial project.

—Teresa Delgado[2]

The Spirit of the Lord is on me, because he has anointed me to proclaim good news to the poor. He has sent me to proclaim freedom for the prisoners and recovery of sight for the blind, to set the oppressed free, to proclaim the year of the Lord's favor.

—Jesus of Nazareth[3]

Mi mestizaje es complicado. My mom is an Anglo from Colorado, a daughter of southern expats born and raised in Jim-and-Jane Crow. My mamaw hailed from South Carolina; my grandpa grew up in north Florida. Both my grandparents were discipled into White supremacist ideologies and practices. Their segregationist families, churches, and schools provided steady diets of White Jesus, White racism, and White Christian nationalism. This was their daily bread. Even when they migrated to Colorado to escape my abusive great-grandfather, my grandparents carried their internalized White supremacy with them. They had no other choice: they were what they ate. And although Colorado's racial climate curbed some of my grandparents' segregationist sensibilities, it left most untouched—and fostered new forms of anti-Indigenous and anti-Mexican racism. Consequently, my mom inherited a unique blend of southern White supremacy and Colorado-style settler colonialism. And she brought it into her marriage with my dad.

My dad's family is from Puerto Rico—*somos boricuas*—the world's oldest current colony.[4] Early in the twentieth century, the United States colonized Puerto Rico while executing its global imperialist project to carry "the white man's burden."[5] Senator Henry Cabot Lodge and Theodore Roosevelt led the charge. In a May 1898 letter to Lodge, Roosevelt wrote, "Give my best love to Nannie, and *do not make peace until we get Porto Rico*."[6] Lodge responded, "Porto Rico is not forgotten and we mean to have it. Unless I am utterly . . . mistaken, the administration is now fully committed to the large policy that we both desire."[7] That year, the Treaty of Paris (1898) placed Puerto Rico under US jurisdiction. Lodge and Roosevelt got their wish. They had conquered and colonized my paternal ancestors.

Imperialists were eager to plunder my paternal ancestors' resources and weaponize Puerto Rico's place in the Antilles. But they balked at incorporating *mi gente y mi isla* because they were not White. Government officials argued that "in the annexation of outlying and distant possessions grave questions will arise from differences of race, habits, laws, and customs of the people." These officials believed that "a false step at this time might be fatal to the development of what Chief Justice Marshall called the 'American Empire.'" Consequently, Congress and the Supreme Court chose to render Puerto Rico an exploitable colony whose inhabitants were "foreign . . . in a domestic sense."[8] So it remains.[9]

I did not know this history growing up. Although learning it is my birthright, it was not part of my inheritance. Neither was Spanish. Instead, I inherited English and myths of US innocence and benevolence that legitimated *mi familia boricua*'s US military service.[10] Crushing poverty from colonial exploitation, early parental deaths, religious persecution for being Protestant, and familial embraces of martial life—these factors spurred *mis abuelos'* decisions to pursue lifelong service in the US Air Force. Hence national myths and Anglocentric assimilation practices in military communities across the country were my dad's dietary staples. So too were theologies that emphasized God forgiving sins in Christ but said nothing about God's disdain for empires or commitments to liberating the oppressed.[11] If my mom and her parents brought a unique blend of White supremacy to my parents' marriage, my dad and *abuelos* brought a colonial mentality infused with internalized racism.[12]

My formal education before graduate school offered little to remediate the generational racism I inherited. The historically and predominantly White schools I attended throughout the northeastern United States perpetuated forms of *organized forgetting*—the intentional, repetitious omitting of certain facts, narratives, and artifacts, and the repetitious presenting of other facts, narratives, and artifacts[13]—that maintained White dominance and Latine subordination. The same was true of the churches I joined. And in all these communities and institutions, I suffered racist experiences: My sixth-grade English honors teacher proclaimed to my classmates and me that I was only in the class to boost racial diversity numbers; wealthy White parents told my teammates and me to return to the prison; a youth leader chastised me during a meeting for voicing concerns about racist ideas I heard in church; and a professor praised the United States' conquest of uncivilized people during the Spanish-American War—such experiences scarred me and kept me from settling for my familial inheritance. To echo W. E. B. Du Bois, "Had it not been for the race problem early thrust upon me and enveloping me, I should have probably been an unquestioning worshipper at the shrine of the established social order and of the economic development into which I was born."[14]

I began acquiring race-conscious resources to heal my colonial wounds in graduate school. During the first year of my MA program at Texas A&M University, I met Tommy J. Curry. When Curry learned I was Puerto Rican, he encouraged me to study Critical Race Theory (CRT), directing me to canonical texts and warning me against straying far from them because White scholars were gentrifying the field.[15] I heeded Curry's counsel a year later. My initial foray into CRT was painful, for it illuminated how little I knew about racialization and White supremacy's histories. My ignorance overwhelmed me. And it sparked a nascent realization: I needed an educational overhaul.

I started overhauling my education at Baylor University.[16] As I began coursework, I launched several self-study programs, including race scholarship. Footnotes were my guides. They offered concise maps of disciplinary literatures and paths to must-read texts. I continued learning these maps and paths while writing a dissertation on Thomas Aquinas. Upon graduating, I was a competent Thomist and race scholar.

Shortly before graduating, I accepted a position to teach courses on race and justice at Wheaton College (IL). The opportunity thrilled and terrified me. I was eager to offer courses that unmasked White supremacy, but I knew that executing this task in a historically and predominantly White Christian college would be immensely challenging. One of these challenges would be confronting the reoccurring thought that, from the institution's perspective, I principally served to provide cover against charges of racism; I was there for racial diversity numbers. The more I considered this challenge, the more a line by Tommy Curry haunted me: "Despite the recent rise in articles by American philosophers willing to deal with race, the sophistication of American philosophy's conceptualizations of American racism continues to lag behind other liberal arts fields committed to similar endeavors." Curry later notes that "many scholars interested in exploring the themes of racism (marginalization, silencing, power, etc.) are taken to be authoritative, regardless of their formal education in the histories of oppressed peoples in the United States, or a functional knowledge of the development of White supremacy within America's geography."[17] The possibility that Curry's words described me was horrifying. I lacked the formal education he championed, deemed my understanding of White supremacy's history mediocre, and most painful, knew I avoided studying how White supremacy had ravaged my family and me. I had reached a reckoning generations in the making—and I knew it. I responded by committing to become an academically respected CRT scholar devoted to healing my colonial wounds. That was 2018, two years before George Floyd's murder and the anti-CRT movements that ensued and two years before I started receiving hate mail.

Teaching to Liberate

I joined Wheaton College's philosophy department the year after it experienced two significant events. First, an external review chastised the department for its lack of racial and gender diversity among its faculty and curriculum. Second, the administration decided not to renew an older White adjunct professor's contract in response to the backlash against a speaker he invited to campus. This decision put the department and administration in a bind, for that adjunct professor was the only philosophy professor who taught courses on race. Recognizing this problem, the provost instructed the department to hire a one-year replacement to teach a course called "Race and Justice." At the same time, she established a new tenure-track line dedicated to political philosophy and the philosophy of race. Two months later, I applied for and received the visiting position. After another round of intensive interviews the following semester, I accepted an offer for the tenure-track position.

The version of "Race and Justice" I inherited operated with a Black-White binary. As the course catalog description explained, "Race and Justice" was "an introduction to philosophy and racial diversity in the United States, focusing on justice and African Americans." Though common, this racial binary inhibits robust understandings of racism.[18] On one hand, Black-White binaries obfuscate the historical truth that racism has involved White-over-Black ideologies and practices, not mere Black-White ones.[19] On the other hand, because human beings construct racist theories and material conditions with relational conceptions of human races—for example, Whites and Blacks are defined in relation to one another and other racial groups—understanding historical and current forms of White supremacy and anti-Blackness requires understanding their racial counterparts (e.g., including anti-Asian, anti-Indigenous, and anti-Latine racism).[20] Consequently, my version of "Race and Justice" needed to avoid a Black-White binary. But it also needed to address three additional, interrelated pedagogical challenges: White ignorance, corrupt theologies, and anti-CRT discipleship.

Scholars have long known that White communities usually suffer from racial illiteracy and indoctrination into racist myths.[21] Jamaican philosopher Charles Mills developed the concept of *White ignorance* to account for both problems.[22] More specifically, White ignorance refers to an aggressive, resistant, group-based ignorance consisting of false beliefs and the absence of true beliefs about racism and White supremacy. Mills clarifies his view with ten additional propositions. He defines White ignorance as

1. A cognitive phenomenon that must be historicized according to a constructivist rather than essentialist theory of race;[23]
2. Distinct from general patterns of ignorance prevalent among people who are White but in whose beliefs race has played no determining role;
3. Consistent with granting that "it will sometimes be very difficult to adjudicate when specific kinds of non-knowing are appropriately categorizable as White ignorance or not";
4. An amalgam of "straightforward racist motivation and more impersonal social-structural causation, which may be operative even if the cognizer in question is not racist";
5. Not confined to White people;
6. Generative, producing other forms of racial ignorance (e.g., the anti-White theories championed in early Black Muslim theologies);
7. Morally laden, including "ignorance of facts with moral implications and moral non-knowings, [and] incorrect judgments about the rights and wrongs of moral situations themselves";
8. One of several privileged, group-based ignorance such as male ignorance;
9. Not uniform across White communities; and
10. Reducible through modes of consciousness raising that highlight the structural, communal, and individual factors which produce and perpetuate it.[24]

People influenced by White ignorance are like those in Plato's cave allegory: they suffer from a cave-like socialization characterized by gross racialized misperceptions and racist ideological bondage.[25] They need help. They need Spirit-empowered consciousness raising that heals their sight, loosens their ideological chains, and brings them to new heights of love of God, self, and neighbor. Put biblically, they need liberation.

Liberation from White ignorance requires confronting a second pedagogical challenge I face: most of my students have inherited immensely corrupt theologies. To echo C. René Padilla, my students frequently have been discipled into an Anglocentric, American-way-of-life Christianity that ensures that "the racist can continue to be a racist, the exploiter can continue to be an exploiter." Versions of Christianity grown in this soil often contain a distorted, hyperspiritualized gospel that focuses almost exclusively on individual forgiveness of sin while saying little or nothing about the Kingdom of God, the Kingdom's social ethic, or the Kingdom's place within cosmic redemption. As Padilla argued, such mutilated gospels "can only be the basis for unfaithful churches, for strongholds of racial and class discrimination, for religious clubs with a message that has no relevance to practical life in the social, the economic, and the political spheres."[26] Put plainly, many of my students need fresh presentations of the wholistically liberating gospel proclaimed and enacted by Jesus of Nazareth.

The recent anti-CRT movements exacerbate the pedagogical challenges of confronting and redressing White ignorance and corrupt theologies. These movements have fed upon and increased White Christian nationalism, deemed discourses about oppression and exploitation "cultural Marxism," and labeled scholarship and practices aimed at resisting and redressing racism and White supremacy "wokeness." Moreover, these movements fill the communities to which many of my students belong. For such students, learning race scholarship and experiencing racialized liberation may come at a great price: ostracization from the communities you love.

My version of "Race and Justice" confronts the Black-White binary, White ignorance, corrupt theologies, and anti-CRT movements through a fifteen-week journey with five stages. First, my students and I cultivate a common language. We read Plato's cave allegory; revisit biblical terms like "gospel" and "oppression";[27] reconsider "race," "whiteness," and "White supremacy";[28] and retrieve Thomas Aquinas's teachings on justice (*iustitia*), injustice (*iniustitia*), and mercy (*misericordia*).[29] Then because a "philosopher must be a student of history . . . to truly understand the projects, resistance, and subtle—but profound—ruptures and challenges waged against the tides of White supremacy,"[30] we proceed through history-steeped sections on anti-Black, anti-Indigenous, anti-Latine, and anti-Asian racism, respectively. Our goal is to grow in justice, love, mercy, and understanding. Thus, our liberating journey enters a eucharistic register that resonates with Mari Matsuda's pledge: "I cannot pretend that I, as a Japanese American, truly know the pain of, say, my Native American sister. But I can pledge to educate myself, so I do not receive her pain in ignorance."[31]

The previous paragraph contains a significant linguistic shift. I moved from writing about "my students" to "my students and I" and "our." This shift is key, for it acknowledges that my course curriculum is not only for my students; it is also for me—for my liberation and healing. I can journey with my students because "I view them from unusual points of vantage. Not as a foreigner do I come, for I am native, not foreign, bone of their thought and flesh of their language."[32] I grew up in an Anglocentric Latine family and attended historically and predominantly White institutions. All housed and cultivated Black-White binaries, White ignorance, and corrupt American-way-of-life theologies. Like my students, I need Spirit-empowered liberation from these evils. Like them, I need God to heal me through this course even five years into teaching it.

Research as Me-Search

Like bell hooks, "I came to theory . . . to grasp what was happening around and within me."[33] I initially studied philosophy because it supported my efforts to answer personal, vexing questions with interdisciplinary resources from across the centuries. I continue to study philosophy for the same reason—despite the bitter truth that "Black, Brown, and Indigenous philosophers have dedicated their lives and careers to educating White philosophers and students, with little to no effect on the composition and disposition of the discipline."[34] Centuries of imperial and patriarchal White supremacist ideologies, practices, and structures undergird present-day professional philosophy. White males still dominate the field. So does White ignorance. But a disciplinary openness to and incentivizing of interdisciplinary research, publications, and teaching provide me sufficient space to ask and answer questions that my life experiences and *mestizaje* thrust upon me.

Throughout my brief professional career, one of my guiding research questions has been "What should sanctification look like in a racialized world?" My early efforts to answer this question have involved retrieval work in Thomistic studies and extended stays in CRT scholarship. But the more I studied CRT, the more I desired to learn Latine and liberation theologies. Thus, I experienced a form of what Orlando Crespo calls an *interactive view* of Christian discipleship; as this scholarship increased my awareness of racist colonial and imperial practices, I craved theologies that named, analyzed, and denounced these evils to promote the love of God, self, and neighbor, and reading these theologies subsequently spurred my desire to grow in consciousness by reading CRT.[35] This interaction brought me to a scholarly crossroads, to another personal reckoning.

Before me were two options: undertake decolonial, CRT-informed research that centers my unique *mestizaje* and colonial wounds or pursue antiracist research dictated by preexisting literature and projects. Academic reward systems and my training inclined me toward the latter; my growing commitment to grace-sustained, liberating self-love pushed me to the former. Accepting this vocational push hurt. It required acknowledging the painful truth that a version of Cherríe L. Moraga's and Gloria Anzaldúa's words were my own: "Daily, we feel the pull and tug of having to choose between which parts of our mothers' heritages we want to claim and wear and which parts have served to cloak us from the knowledge of ourselves."[36] Accepting this vocational push also required acknowledging that I avoided researching my unique *mestizaje* and colonial wounds as a coping response: I did not want to see, let alone confront, the festering wounds that island Puerto Ricans had inflicted upon me. Teresa Delgado partially voices my pain: "I claim my heritage as a Puerto Rican; I am rejected as such by many on the island who believe that I have lost the right to assert such ethnicity when my dominant language is English and I am privileged by all the benefits of life on the mainland."[37] Sifting through one's familial inheritance hurts. Dealing with diasporic rejections compounds the pain.

As I embrace my evolving research trajectory, James Baldwin comes to mind. He knew "the past is all that makes the present coherent, and further, that the past will remain horrible for exactly as long as we refuse to assess it honestly."[38] He made a similar point midway through *The Fire Next Time*: "The paradox—and a fearful paradox it is—is that the American Negro can have no future anywhere, on any continent, as long as he is unwilling to accept his past. To accept one's past—one's history—is not the same thing as drowning in it; it is learning how to use it. An invented past can never be used; it cracks and crumbles under the pressures of life like clay in a season of drought."[39] Whether general or race-specific, Baldwin's call to honestly assess the past and put it to use sings to me. And to date, it has been a guiding star to a richer understanding of myself and Jesus, the colonized first-century Palestinian Jew whose death on an imperial cross secured my healing liberation. He is the one calling me to walk this God-ordained scholarly path with the Spirit.

Mentoring and Institutional Service

Since my first day at Wheaton College, my department chairs and dean have encouraged me to say no in order to say yes. Because they want me to pursue life-giving teaching, research, and service, they counsel me to say no to requests that would make that difficult and yes to opportunities that would foster it. Unfortunately, few racialized minorities receive this counsel from their institutional superiors. I am privileged to be one of those who do.

Empowered to say no, I have limited my nonteaching institutional commitments to mentoring students and faculty standing committees. Wheaton incentivizes both by including them in the "promotable skills" portions of our yearly, tenure, and promotion evaluations. And whereas many colleges do not really care about these parts of academic life, Wheaton does, and evaluators review my colleagues and me accordingly.

I mentor students communally and individually. Communally, I have led several book groups and served as a faculty advisor for Wheaton's Latine student group, *Unidad Cristiana*. Both groups have selected and reviewed race-conscious literature that Wheaton courses have omitted.[40] As a faculty advisor, my most crucial mentoring contribution has been supporting students and amplifying their voices.

One of our hardest experiences has been the group's response to a racist meme that pictured several of us worshiping on stage during the first-ever *Unidad*-led chapel. Seeing this violation was rough. This was followed by an ensuing four-month Title IX case, laden with fresh racial trauma and retraumatization. The entire process was wretched. Enduring it forced the students and me to value self-care. We learned that Audre Lorde is right: "Caring for myself is not self-indulgence, it is self-preservation, and that is an act of political warfare."[41] Our addition: Latine self-care manifests the liberating Kingdom of God in historically and predominantly White institutions.

The communal suffering I endured with *Unidad* drove me to reimagine individual mentoring. Wheaton houses extensive resources for professional development, academic or otherwise. But it has few individuals or programs students trust to help them navigate crises or catastrophes. Time and again, the students who ask me for mentorship are really asking these questions: "Professor Cartagena, will you join me in my sufferings? Will you help me name what I have experienced? Will you help me heal? Will you provide me a safe space to think through the evils without and within? Will you offer me counsel without a White gaze? Will you help me find a Jesus who celebrates women and empowers them to lead? Will you journey with me as I come out as queer? Will you help me repent of my disdain for the poor? Will you walk with me as I confront my internalized racism?" Across race, class, and gender, students I mentor ultimately seek my sustained assistance with these pressing issues. They are searching for health and the renewing Spirit of Christ in a world filled with calamities. These truths, not a disciplinary agenda, inform my mentoring.

My commitments to liberating, race-conscious pedagogy, decolonial scholarship, and mentoring that promotes health amid crises and catastrophes set fixed limits for my service on standing committees. So does my dearth of administration gifts. Consequently, I have said no to administration-heavy committees and yes to committees that support Wheaton College without requiring that I suppress my commitments and pretend to be someone I am not. Not everyone has this option. Indeed, many Latines are "voluntold" to join time- and energy-intensive committees to diversify them. There are many ways to rob Peter to pay Paul.

A closing word. Growing up, I regularly faced the temptation to accommodate White preferences by pacifying non-White righteous indignation. I still face this temptation in my family of origin. And I face it at Wheaton College. The academic version often goes like this: "Dr. Cartagena, the minority students are having a hard time and growing angry. Could you . . . ?" Rare is the request that contains any recognition of institutional or personal culpability for perpetuating racism against these students. Common is the call to help the students "feel better." That is not mentoring, nor is it true institutional service. That is racist-enabling pacification. There is no health there. And I respond accordingly.

Notes

1　Ada María Isasi-Díaz, *En la lucha / In the Struggle: Elaborating a Mujerista Theology*, 10th anniversary ed. (Minneapolis, MN: Fortress Press, 2004), xi.

2　Teresa Delgado, *A Puerto Rican Decolonial Theology: Prophesy Freedom* (New York: Springer, 2017), 13.

3　Luke 4:18–19 NIV.

4　José Trías Monge, *Puerto Rico: The Trials of the Oldest Colony in the World*, rev. ed. (New Haven, CT: Yale University Press, 1999).

5　Rudyard Kipling, "The White Man's Burden," *McClure's Magazine*, February 1899. Lodge and Roosevelt agreed that Kipling's poem made "good sense from the expansion point of view."

6　Quoted in Karl Wagenheim and Olga Jimenez de Wagenheim, eds., *The Puerto Ricans: A Documentary History*, 2nd ed. (Princeton, NJ: Markus Wiener, 2002), 89. Emphasis in original.

7　Monge, *Puerto Rico*, 89.

8　*Downs v. Bidwell*, 182 U.S. 244 (1901).

9　For why the "promotion" to "commonwealth" did not substantially change Puerto Rico's colonial status, see Ed Morales, *Colonialism, Exploitation, and the Betrayal of Puerto Rico* (New York: Bold Type Books, 2019).

10　On "myths of innocence," see Justo González, *Mañana: Christian Theology from a Hispanic Perspective* (Nashville, TN: Abingdon Press, 1990), 38–42. On pressures that Puerto Ricans face to join the US military, see Juan Gonzalez, *Harvest of Empire: A History of Latin America* (New York: Penguin, 2000).

11　For an extended treatment of God's disdain for empires and commitments to oppressed people, see Antonio González, *God's Reign and the End of Empires* (Miami, FL: Convivium, 2012).

12　Martinican decolonial psychiatrist Frantz Fanon wrote thus about colonial mentalities, "Colonialism is not satisfied merely with holding a people in its grip and emptying the native's brain of all form and content. By a kind of perverted logic, it turns to the past of the oppressed people, and distorts, disfigures, and destroys it." See Fanon, *The Wretched of the Earth* (New York: Grove Press, 1963), 210–11. For a Latine discussion about colonial mentalities and internalized racism, see Laura M. Padilla, "Social and Legal Repercussions of Latinos' Colonized Mentality," *University of Miami Law Review* 53 (1999): 769–85.

13　The phrase "organized forgetting" is from Kendall Thomas, "*Rouge et Noir* Reread: A Popular Constitutional History of the Angelo Herndon Case," *Southern California Law Review* 65 (1992): 2664.

14 W. E. B. Du Bois, "Dusk of Dawn," in *Writings*, ed. Nathan Huggins (New York: Library of America, 1987), 573.

15 Tommy J. Curry, "Canonizing the Critical Race Artifice: An Analysis of Philosophy's Gentrification of Critical Race Theory," in *The Routledge Companion to the Philosophy of Race*, ed. Paul Taylor, Linda Alcoff, and Luvell Anderson (New York: Routledge, 2017), 349–62.

16 The next three paragraphs come from a forthcoming essay with *Comment Magazine*.

17 Tommy J. Curry, "Concerning the Underspecialization of Race Theory in American Philosophy: How the Exclusion of Black Sources Affects the Field," *Pluralist* 5, no. 1 (2010): 53.

18 For an excellent discussion and refutation of Black-White binary thinking, see Juan F. Perea, "The Black/White Binary Paradigm of Race," *California Law Review* 85 (1997): 1213–58.

19 See, for example, Winthrop Jordan, *White over Black: American Attitudes toward the Negro, 1550–1812* (Chapel Hill: University of North Carolina Press, 2012).

20 For an extended treatment of this point, see Richard Delgado, "Derrick Bell's Toolkit—Fit to Dismantle That Famous House?," *New York University Law Review* 75, no. 2 (2000): 283–307.

21 On White racial illiteracy, see Lani Guinier, "From Racial Liberalism to Racial Literacy: Brown v. Board of Education and the Interest-Divergence Dilemma," *Journal of American History* 91 (2004): 92–118. On White indoctrination into racist myths, see Joe R. Feagin, *The White Racial Frame: Centuries of Racial Framing and Counter-Framing*, 2nd ed. (New York: Routledge, 2013).

22 See Charles W. Mills, "White Ignorance," in *Race and Epistemologies of Ignorance*, ed. Shannon Sullivan and Nancy Tuana (Albany: State University of New York Press, 2007), 11–38; and Mills, "Global White Ignorance," in *Routledge International Handbook of Ignorance Studies*, ed. Matthias Gross and Linsey McGoey (New York: Routledge, 2015), 217–27.

23 Constructivist theories contend that races are social inventions rather than biologically real; essentialist theories affirm the opposite. On this distinction, see Ian Haney López, "The Social Construction of Race: Some Observations on Illusion, Fabrication, and Choice," *Harvard Civil Rights–Civil Liberties Law Review* 29, no. 1 (1994): 1–62.

24 Mills, "White Ignorance," 20–23.

25 See Plato's *Republic*, Book 7.

26 C. René Padilla, *Mission between the Times: Essays on the Kingdom*, rev. ed. (Carlisle, UK: Langham Monographs, 2013), 55.

27 See Padilla, *Mission*; and Elsa Támez, *Bible of the Oppressed*, trans. Matthew J. O'Connell (Eugene, OR: Wipf & Stock, 1982).

28 See López, "Social Construction of Race"; and Robert P. Jones, *White Too Long: The Legacy of White Supremacy in American Christianity* (New York: Simon & Schuster, 2020).

29 See Thomas Aquinas's *Summa Theologiae*.

30 Tommy J. Curry, *Another White Man's Burden: Josiah Royce's Quest for a Philosophy of White Racial Empire* (Albany: State University of New York Press, 2018), xx.

31 Mari Matsuda, "When the First Quail Calls: Multiple Consciousness as Jurisprudential Method," *Women's Rights Law Reporter* 14, nos. 2–3 (1992): 300.

32 W. E. B. Du Bois, "Darkwater: Voices from within the Veil," in Huggins, *Writings*, 923.

33 bell hooks, *Teaching to Transgress: Education as the Practice of Freedom* (New York: Routledge, 1994), 59.

34 Tommy J. Curry and Gwenetta Curry, "On the Perils of Race Neutrality and Anti-Blackness: Philosophy as an Irreconcilable Obstacle to (Black) Thought," *American Journal of Economics and Sociology* 77, nos. 3–4 (2018): 659.

35 Orlando Crespo, *Being Latino in Christ: Finding Wholeness in Your Ethnic Identity* (Downers Grove, IL: InterVarsity Press, 2003), 90.

36 Cherríe L. Moraga and Gloria Anzaldúa, *This Bridge Called My Back: Writings by Radical Women of Color*, 4th ed. (Albany: State University of New York Press, 2015), 19.

37 Delgado, *Puerto Rican Decolonial Theology*, 180.

38 James Baldwin, *Collected Essays*, ed. Toni Morrison (New York: Library of America, 1998), 7.

39 James Baldwin, *The Fire Next Time*, Modern Library ed. (1962; repr., New York: Penguin Random House, 2021), 67.

40 Examples include Ian Haney López, *White by Law: The Legal Construction of Race*, 10th anniversary ed. (New York: New York University Press, 2006); and Cornel West, *Prophesy Deliverance! An Afro-American Revolutionary Christian*, anniversary ed. (Louisville, KY: Westminster John Knox Press, 2002).

41 Audre Lorde, *A Burst of Light: And Other Essays* (1988; repr., Mineola, NY: Ixia Press, 2017), 130.

6

UNDERCOVER MEXICANA

From Heritage Denier to Bilingual Profesora

VERÓNICA A. GUTIÉRREZ

I sat on a wrought iron bench in a small plaza enjoying the crispness of February. It was my first visit to Guanajuato City, a hilly, cobblestoned university town, and I wanted to remember this place, which I had longed to visit since I was a child. A doctoral student in colonial Mexican history at UCLA ("la ookla," as locals call it), I was living in México for my research year on a Fulbright-García Robles scholarship (*beca*) studying native participation in the Christianization process. My research site was the Indigenous-Christian city of Cholula in Puebla, nearly three hundred miles away, and I had bumped along in taxis and buses for hours through mountain passes and up and down hills to arrive at this mining town.

Above me loomed the bell towers of the seventeenth-century Basilica of Our Lady of Guanajuato, which housed an image of the Virgin and Child, a gift from Holy Roman Emperor Charles V and his son, Philip II, in 1557. Gazing at the church's facade, painted yellow like so many colonial-era churches in México, I recalled stories my mother had told me about her father, who had grown up in a nearby village but had succumbed to lung cancer before I was born. A laborer on the railroads, he was a devout Catholic who attended daily mass in south Texas, where she grew up. On nights she passed his room en route to the outhouse, she would see his kneeling shadow beside the bed. He had instilled our faith in her, and she had instilled it in me.

Mi abuelito had, I knew, fled Guanajuato during the violence of the Mexican Revolution when he was around twelve, walking alongside a cart with his sister and her husband toward a better life in Texas. He had little formal education, yet he supported his family of twelve by working multiple jobs and building their home. My mother remembers running through the half-built house with her siblings and jumping off the back porch.

As I sat thinking about the complicated events in my family history leading me to this moment, I felt a presence join me on the bench. I knew, in an instant, that it was my grandfather. Hardly daring to breathe, I waited.

In the silence that followed, I felt my sweet *abuelito* telling me that he was happy that I had come to Guanajuato at long last. He let me know he was delighted that I had taken an interest in my past, in *our* past, and that my decision to pursue a PhD in colonial Mexican history and to master Spanish filled him with pride. Most importantly, he said that he loved me even though we had never met.

When I felt his presence cover my hand with his, I wept.

I come from a family of educators. My parents, now retired teachers, taught elementary, junior high, and high school during careers spanning Texas and Arizona. My sister knew from the age of six that she would be a teacher, and I have been teaching since 2001. My daughter, the third generation, shows aptitude as a teacher. Teaching is in our blood, I tell her. From my earliest days, my parents stressed the importance of education, which I've passed along to my children.

We are *Tejanos*. My father grew up in Zapata in a small house with dirt floors on a plot of land so close to the border that he could see México from his front yard. The Gutiérrezes arrived with a land grant in hand from the Spanish Crown to colonize northern New Spain. The land shifted around them—colonial México became independent México, the Republic of Texas, and the United States. The border crossed us. My mother grew up two hours away in Harlingen with her big, boisterous family. My parents met when my dad took a teaching job in my mom's hometown and had her youngest brother in class.

After marrying and settling between their hometowns, my bilingual, public schoolteacher parents adopted English as our home language so that we would not speak with an accent. They hoped to avoid the prejudice they had endured growing up at the border, particularly my father, who remembers signs on restaurants and stores declaring "No dogs or Mexicans allowed."

After my second birthday, we moved to Phoenix, where two of my mother's sisters had already settled with their families. The Texas cousins spoke Spanish. The Arizona cousins did not. Indeed, some of my Arizona cousins could not pronounce our surname because they could not roll their Rs. To afford Catholic school, my parents taught classes before and after school in the summers. My siblings and I rode the bus to our school, an hour each way.

Bus Ride through Guadalupe

The faded orange school bus bumped along the neighborhood one balmy morning, pale light slanting onto students dozing against green hardback seats. I sat alone, lost in my imagination. The bus heaved its girth into a wide right turn, ambling past a "Welcome to Guadalupe" sign and crossing into a village of Mexican immigrants. Though I didn't know it then, this was a community of Yaqui native people who fled Sonora during the Mexican Revolution, just as my grandfather had fled Guanajuato.

As the bus maneuvered the compacted clay roads, dogs passed dangerously near the wheels. Small homes assembled of plywood, concrete bricks, and corrugated metal sheets passed our windows. Abandoned cars sat in yards overgrown with weeds. Stopping beside a simple, well-tended residence, the bus squeaked open its doors, and two sisters climbed aboard, bringing a halo of dust in their wake. The older one was in my sister's class, and the younger one was in mine.

As we pulled away, kids began yelling insults out the window. Lurching out of the neighborhood, we passed a wraparound drive-through liquor store called "The Circle B." One of the loudest kids, thinking himself especially clever, filled the window frame with his face, sharply drew in his breath, and shrieked: "I know why you call it the Circle B! Stupid Mexicans! Because you don't know any further in the alphabet!"

The boy's shrill voice hung heavy in the air, his ugly words contrasting with the lulling sound of the bus's wheels gliding once again along the paved blacktop.

I hunched into my seat. *I* was not Mexican. We were poor, but we weren't dirt poor. My family lived in a normal house. My dad kept the front yard clear of weeds. We had two cars, and they both worked. Our streets were paved, and dogs walked on leashes. No, *I* was not Mexican. I would never be Mexican.

As a child, I was an avid storyteller. I would spend hours crafting stories in the room I shared with my sister. Sitting under an open window at my dad's little college writing desk, I would write furiously, producing piles of stories, some of which I illustrated. Initially focusing on talking animals, I eventually began writing about my family, the family I wanted us to be. I named myself Agnes and my mother Rachel. I ditched Gutiérrez in favor of Smith, the most American surname I knew. My parents spoke perfect English in my stories, and I had light skin and eyes. We had a pool and a big, loyal dog. I wrote what I believed to be the typical American story because I was convinced that being American meant being White.

My mother made several attempts to teach us Spanish. Though my parents addressed us in Spanish at home, we responded in English. We understood, but we could not communicate; my children are the same. On spring afternoons, with the screen door open to let in the cool breeze and the sounds of neighborhood kids beckoning us outside, we would sit around the dining room table reciting the Spanish alphabet after our mother. We practiced rolling our Rs and played Mexican bingo, covering the images with pinto beans when my mother called out "el alacrán" or "la chalupa." But our hearts were outside with our English-speaking friends, and eventually, my mother grew weary of the battle. Even a few years of *ballet folklórico* (Mexican folk dancing) were not enough to embrace our culture. If anything, the other mothers' rapid cadence frightened me, unlike my mother's calm, deliberate Spanish.

By the time I entered my classical Catholic high school, I was thoroughly Americanized. Or so I believed. I was not Mexican and cringed if someone hinted I was. When classmates complained about the Mexicans who lingered in the alleys near the high school, fixing their cars as they blared *ranchero* music, I would think: *They* are Mexican. *I* am American.

A move to the St. Ignatius Institute at the Jesuit University of San Francisco shifted my attitude when I began studying Spanish. My professor, a *Castellana*, integrated culture and history, piquing my interest in the richness of my past. I began listening to Spanish radio and buying Spanish pop CDs. Within a few months, I decided to connect more directly with my heritage.

La Raza Unida

Late afternoon shadows played out a story on the walls of Hays Healy Hall at the University of San Francisco that October afternoon. Inside, I stood in my room, staring at the mirror filled with anticipation. I had decided to attend a meeting of the campus club La Raza Unida. After years of denying my *mexicanidad* and refusing to speak "that language"—as I supposedly retorted as a child—I was ready to embrace my culture. It was a monumental decision, and I felt more proud than nervous: proud to have such rich cultural roots; proud to call myself Latina.

Walking briskly up a steep incline dubbed Cardiac Hill, I arrived out of breath at McLaren Hall, and the corridors confused me. I sat just as the student leader started introductions, and on my turn, I pronounced my name proudly in Spanish, *Verónica*, the way my mother did, the way my Spanish professor did.

When everyone broke into rapid, cadenced Spanglish, I became lost. The student leader kept mentioning the *altar* (stress on the second syllable), and what kind of decorations we should prepare. *Altar?* I didn't understand, though if I had seen it spelled, I would have realized he meant "altar." The club was planning its annual Day of the Dead altar, a Mexican tradition honoring deceased family members, on November 2, All Souls Day. I had studied *Día de los muertos* and was excited to celebrate it. Perhaps in a few months, I would be chatting easily in Spanglish.

By the time the meeting ended, however, I wondered if I belonged. Everyone seemed to know one another. No one seemed to notice me. No one turned to speak to me. I stood in a corner uncertainly. Moving toward a group of girls, I stopped when one of them declared loudly, "I just hate when Latinas claim to be Latina when they don't speak Spanish, because clearly they are not." As the other girls nodded, I turned and slipped out the door unnoticed. I would never again attend another meeting. Clearly, I didn't belong. Clearly, I had no right to be Latina.

In the fall of my senior year, my Great Books honors program offered a seminar on warfare. We read José María Gironella's 1953 opus, *The Cypresses Believe in God*, set during the Spanish Civil War, and I found myself looking at an image of my own family. Carmen Elgázu, a strong, proud, deeply Catholic woman whose very presence anchored the family, was my mother. The interactions of this family mirrored my own, and for the first time, I realized that stories like mine could and *did* exist in literature.

I began reading more widely. Inspired to write about my family, I landed a spot in a master of fine arts program in creative nonfiction at the Pennsylvania State University. In Pennsylvania, not only was I exotic, but the cultural and geographic distance from home provided me with the clarity I needed to write about my past. My MFA thesis, *Separated by Faith: Memoirs of a Traditional Catholic Daughter*, explores our family's faith as shaped by my mother.

As I wrote, I realized how little I knew about my own history. Why, in particular, were we Catholic? I enrolled in a Latin American History graduate seminar, and at the course's end, the professor—renowned scholar Matthew Restall—encouraged me to become a historian. I insisted that I was a writer, and he asked, "What are historians if not writers?" After reading documents penned by vanquished peoples in his undergraduate course, Culture of the Spanish Conquest, I was hooked. Realizing that Cholollan (Cholula) became an important Christian evangelization center following a 1519 massacre, I wondered how a people slaughtered by Christians could embrace Christianity. Restall encouraged me to study what no scholar had.

To my delight, UCLA accepted me to their doctoral program with five years of funding. Me, a creative writer with limited training as a historian! With excitement and trepidation, I moved back to California to study the origins of Mexican Catholicism among classmates who were predominantly

Mexican. Ours was a supportive program; we shared books, read one another's papers, shared apartments in México City in the summer, and trekked together to the archives. I learned from my classmates—especially the women, one of whom was a Zapoteca from Oaxaca—about the varied shades of *mexicanidad*. I realized I had every right to be Latina.

Many years later, I filed for my PhD on a Monday in June, and that Saturday, my husband proposed. I had already landed a job at Azusa Pacific University for the fall, but he insisted on waiting until I finished my dissertation so our wedding would not distract me. He was waiting to ask me as Dr. Gutiérrez; the son of Mexican and Panamanian immigrants, he recognized the significance of being the first in my family to obtain a PhD.

Navigating Teaching

"What are you?" a male student asked me after class during my first year of graduate school at the Pennsylvania State University; I had moved to Pennsylvania mere weeks before the September 11 terrorist attacks and began teaching right away. Startled by the question, I paused, but there wasn't any trace of disrespect in his expression, merely curiosity.

"Do you mean, what is my ethnicity?" I asked pleasantly, zipping up my satchel and moving it off the desk so that I held its full weight in my right hand.

"Yeah, like where you're from and stuff." He gazed at me expectantly, and I gazed back. He stood holding the strap of a blue backpack. He was African American and I wondered if he felt a shared kinship with me, if our position as two minorities in a predominantly White central Pennsylvania town prompted him to formulate the question as he had without the usual lead-in.

"My ancestors are from México," I told him. "But we've been in the United States for several generations."

"Oh." He smiled. "That's what I thought, that you were Spanish because of your name." I smiled back and nodded. Actually, I am Mexican American, and my first language is English, but I knew what he meant. He turned and walked out of the classroom, and I followed.

Throughout my career, I had students admit that they had hesitated to take my classes because they worried, based on my name, that I would speak poor English. What irony, no? For the one who had denied her *mexicanidad* and felt unworthy of calling herself Latina to be cast as culturally different. I would inevitably encounter students like me who grew up in bilingual families but did not speak Spanish. They'd be surprised when I admitted that I did not learn Spanish until I was thirty and living in México and that I remained self-conscious of my accent.

Despite being raised by educators, I didn't know how to teach. Despite the pedagogical training I received at Penn State, I didn't understand my job as a graduate instructor. I would read the material at night, then walk into my morning class saying, "The reading was pretty self-explanatory. Are there any questions?" No wonder my teaching evaluations were low.

We were not TAs at Penn State; we had our own classrooms. It was there that I became a teacher, learning how to plan a syllabus, design assignments, lead discussions, conference with students, and most importantly, be pedagogically flexible. For the latter, I credit a graduate course, Writer in the Community, which had a teaching component outside the university. Each week I bused to Brookline Village Retirement Community to teach memoir to five students aged seventy-five (born 1926) to ninety-five (born 1906), mostly Penn State alumni.

I was twenty-five, and these women taught me much more than I taught them. One wrote stories about life with her strong, vibrant husband; when she refused to continue her memoir past his debilitating heart attack (a year before I was born), I realized that the man who sat silently in a wheelchair beside her every week was the same man. A math professor with an MPhil and DPhil from the Imperial College in London who had helped wash dishes after Elizabeth I's coronation appointed herself my advisor, a guide to navigating academia as a woman. My oldest student shared details about doing household chores without modern machines while wearing a corset. We had fun discussing their lives, sharing stories, writing, and reading our work. Those ten weeks taught me compassion, flexibility, how to navigate personal history, and most importantly, that teaching is about learning. May all those lovely ladies rest in peace.

I loved having my own classroom and disliked being a TA at UCLA; even so, I was gratified when female students, mostly Latina, would approach me timidly after class to say I inspired them. As a former heritage denier, their words inspired *me*. These types of interactions continued when I took a year's leave to teach a 4/4 course load as a visiting assistant history professor at Loyola Marymount University; I looked so young that everyone mistook me for an undergrad as I crossed campus. One memorable night in History of México, the students mutinied, claiming a lack of preparation for the midterm. I walked out to print the exam and called my veteran teacher mother, who encouraged me to follow my instincts. I declared that my classroom was a dictatorship, not a democracy, and that we would take the midterm. When submitting their exams, students sheepishly acknowledged that it was indeed fair. I nodded silently, grateful to have trusted myself and maintained authority in the classroom. A student from México whispered as she handed me the exam that she admired how I handled the class.

By the time I accepted a position as Azusa Pacific University's first and only Latin America historian in 2012, I was a seasoned educator with experience teaching in two English departments, a history department, and a graduate program. I married during Thanksgiving, my first semester in the Department of History and Political Science. As I suffered through three increasingly difficult pregnancies, my colleagues selflessly took on extra duties. Most of my chair and deans were women and supported me. Indeed, despite three maternity leaves, I received my promotion to associate professor in the same semester as colleagues who entered my year. My four-year-old daughter was in class with me, coloring quietly in a corner, when my dean and chair burst into the room with flowers to announce my promotion. I was proud that my sweet girl witnessed her mama realizing her dreams.

Despite being APU's only Latin Americanist, I struggled to fill my specialty classes, which highlighted the Indigenous perspective. I could not find a way to connect with Latino students, and I met with the Latin American Student Association and advertised in the modern languages department to no avail. I unexpectedly shared another aspect of my identity, however. Because I taught courses centered on evangelization, my mostly Protestant students learned the nuances of Catholic sacramental theology.

By my final year, I was operating in a flipped classroom, recording my lectures and employing a Socratic approach to discussion. Inspired by the challenge of writing a children's book for Ignatius Press about sixteenth-century native visionary Juan Diego—the first rendition related from an Indigenous perspective set against the backdrop of historical 1530s México City—I assigned students historical fiction. The results were impressive, both scholarly and creative.

For years I'd had honors students in my classes, and we would talk about the lack of Latin American writers in their curriculum. In my final year, the Honors College dean, looking to incorporate more voices, invited me to lecture on Azuela's *The Underdogs: A Novel of the Mexican Revolution*, asking if I could recommend additional readings from Latin America. Weeks later, I had a similar request from the Angelicum Academy, a classical Catholic homeschooling program looking to launch its online Great Books program in Spanish. I had so far avoided teaching in Spanish at APU because I was afraid. God had been calling me for two years toward Catholic education, however, and this time, he nudged me. The day Angelicum emailed asking me to direct their new program, my children and I knelt in thanksgiving.

Navigating Research

Throughout my career, I've been committed to challenging the myths pervading native peoples of the Americas, fortunate that APU had various mechanisms in place providing course releases for research. My scholarship, in many ways, reflects my conflicted identity: specializing in the origins of Mexican Catholicism has allowed me to understand myself, my faith, and my past more profoundly. Even so, upon arriving at UCLA, I encountered the assumption that I was a pious Catholic girl doing pious Catholic history. A classmate from México City, who had worked as a journalist in France, was particularly derogatory, declaring that only idiots espoused Catholicism. In response, our advisor paired us on a conference panel; hearing my paper exploring sacramental confession among the Nahuas in sixteenth-century México convinced my classmate I was a serious scholar.

My research agenda coalesced during the summers I spent researching in Cholula. Participating in processions and enveloping myself in Mexican Catholicism provided as much insight into local culture as local history.[1] I lived with Mexican housemates on the site of a *teocalli* (god-house), converted into a Franciscan guesthouse, under the supervision of a friar who served as headmaster of a school three blocks away; heavy summer rains would unearth ancient pottery shards and obsidian pieces in the backyard. I participated in the life of the house, washing dishes, eating *pan dulce* and *chocolate* in the evenings, and sitting silently through long *comidas* every Sunday. During one such meal, I slipped into the courtyard where the friar's six-year-old nephew was playing. Sitting companionably next to me, he showed me his *piñones* (pine nuts), interrupting our conversation to ask incredulously, "Why don't you know how to talk?!" I laughed and explained that I spoke English very well, but I was learning Spanish. Eager to assist, he led me about the courtyard, my teacher, a moment uniting me with the colonial Franciscans I studied who learned Nahuatl by playing with children.

In 2017, APU invited me to be one of seven featured speakers for its live-streamed TEDx event. Glancing over the list of invited colleagues, I couldn't help but wonder if I were the token Latina. Mentioning my misgivings to another invitee, a neuroscientist whose accomplishments had been broadcast in the university magazine and featured on the website, she looked at me in surprise, saying she would never have thought to ask, since my scholarly reputation was well established at APU. Seven months pregnant, I teetered on pink high heels as I spoke about my beloved Cholula, my husband cheering me from the audience.[2]

I stumbled into my association with the Conference on Faith and History (CFH), a community of mostly evangelical Christian historians that altered my career trajectory. While interviewing for APU, I attended a CFH lunch to meet other APU historians and decided to join. With few Latin American scholars or Catholic members, leadership took notice, inviting me to provide a plenary address at the 2016 CFH meeting, then in 2019 to co-lead a professional development tour for its Latin American initiative to Indigenous-Christian sites in México City, Puebla, Cholula, Huejotzingo, and Tonantzintla.[3] We ended the tour in México City with mass at the Basilica of Our Lady of Guadalupe, which houses a miraculous image of the Virgin who appeared as a native woman to Indigenous visionary Juan Diego in 1531. In the final moments of the tour, we gathered in a circle holding hands beneath the shadow of a figure of Pope St. John Paul II to pray. Before I could step away, participants thanked me for making myself vulnerable by sharing my faith in what became a profoundly spiritual tour.

Five months later, I returned to Cholula as a plenary speaker for a symposium commemorating the five-hundredth anniversary of the Cholula massacre.[4] Giving my first academic paper in Spanish, in the place where I mastered Spanish, while commemorating an event that launched my career as a historian during my MFA days at Penn State felt divinely ordained. After decades of questioning my *mexicanidad* and apologizing for my Spanish, at that moment, I belonged.

Navigating Mentoring

After seeing how students, especially Latinas, responded to me during graduate school, I sought to become an active mentor at APU. Fortuitously, in my first year, a Latina professor launched a program matching faculty mentors with Gen1 students of similar backgrounds. APU provided prepaid hospitality cards, so I mentored Latinas over coffee or Thai food. I also unofficially mentored students during my six years as APU's director of undergraduate research, some of whom did not know how to properly engage with a professor via email or craft a professional funding application. I would invite these students to meet with me in my office or at the campus coffee shop. Mentoring was not part of my duties, but guiding the next generation of students toward success was too important an opportunity to ignore.

I found other ways to mentor students. Successfully navigating APU's mechanisms for research funding, I hired ten Spanish-speaking research assistants—mostly Gen1 Latinas—to assist with my Spanish documents. Beyond a line on a CV rendering them more competitive for grad school, my research assistants gained insight into scholarly production and confidence in their professionalism. I also mentored two undergraduates at La Universidad de las Américas-Puebla in Cholula whom I met while giving a talk at UDLAP's Franciscan Library. A colleague from Puebla who completed his doctoral work in the United States supervised them in the archives as they retrieved, organized, transcribed, analyzed, and translated documents. Now as director of the Great Books program en español for the Angelicum Academy, I teach and mentor Spanish-speaking high school students from the United States and Latin America.

Navigating Service/Administration

Because I had three maternity leaves, I was slow to take on service beyond founding and advising our department's chapter of Phi Alpha Theta, the national history honor society. Yet no one questioned my dedication. In 2016, when APU's director of undergraduate research stepped down, my chair encouraged me to apply. Under my guidance, three of my students had been accepted to present their research papers at the Conference on Faith and History. As I advanced through the interviews, I realized how much I wanted the appointment. Receiving it connected me with our brightest undergraduate researchers and their faculty mentors.

During my six years in this directorship, I transformed the Office of Undergraduate Research (consisting of only me) from a little-known entity into a widely recognized program, largely due to a dedicated supervisor, the executive director of the Office of Research and Grants, and a dependable administrative assistant who would answer my questions almost before I asked them. Primarily responsible for awarding undergraduate conference travel funds and overseeing our annual research funding competition, I also wrote a history of the undergraduate research program, redesigned the one-page website—which had privileged scientific research—into a multipage, multidisciplinary resource, and launched the Undergraduate Research Showcase, a platform for students and mentors to discuss the challenges and benefits of their research experience. I succeeded because of consistent support from the vice provost for undergraduate affairs, the vice provost for graduate programs and research, and the Office of Research and Grants.

During the COVID-19 closures and remote teaching of 2020–21, the outgoing project director of APU's first National Endowment for the Humanities–Hispanic-Serving Institution (NEH-HSI) grant contacted me with an intriguing opportunity. He was leaving APU, and the Provost's Office tasked him with finding a replacement. My status as one of only a few high-producing Latina scholars on faculty, my five years of experience as director of undergraduate research, and my position as APU's first and only Latin America historian rendered me ideally qualified to direct our Summer Bridge program for incoming Gen1 students. Despite the prestige associated with NEH, I hesitated to accept the position while overseeing my children's remote education and teaching online, but the associate provost assured me of her support. The former project director left APU, and I replaced him as director of Bridge and Launch programs.

I assumed the directorship one year into a two-year grant and six months later launched a successful fully remote program in a virtual space I designed on GatherTown. In our virtual assembly on the final day, I listened proudly to our Gen1 students share their research and affirm how the program had provided a critical bridge for their entry to college, despite being remote. Even so, the stress of the role was affecting my health, so I pushed back against the workload, asking my supervisor for release from the one-unit Launch program, which the Provost's Office approved. I was pleased that I had advocated for myself, but then, over the summer, my direct report became the dean of theology.

Under my new supervisor, I did not enjoy the same level of consistent support and became uncomfortable pursuing the role with its change of direction and responsibilities. By the end of the semester, I resigned, while continuing to work with my contact in the Office of Research and Grants to submit the annual NEH report. The Bridge experience galvanized my transition out of APU, something I had been contemplating for a while.

When I received my new contract (APU does not offer tenure), I could not bring myself to sign it. Contracts are always due on April 15, which fell that year on Good Friday. I decided to engage in intensive prayer with my family over Holy Week, all five of us attending Vespers or Divine Liturgy every night at a nearby Russian-Greek Catholic Church. The answer was clear by the Great Vespers of Entombment: God was calling me in a new direction.

<hr />

August 15, 2022, the feast of the Immaculate Conception of the Blessed Virgin Mary, was my last official day at APU, and I awoke feeling down for all I was giving up. My three children made the hour commute to campus with me and helped pack up, lock my office for the last time, and return my laptop. Their presence reminded me of all that I was gaining by leaving. I snapped a photo of them posing by the APU sign before we left, the same sign where ten years earlier I had posed with my then fiancé after signing my contract. How much had changed in a decade.

I now serve as director of the Great Books program en español for the Angelicum Academy, a Catholic homeschooling program. My job has placed me among classical Catholic educators, a return to a world I left twenty years ago when I graduated from the St. Ignatius Institute, a Catholic Great Books program at the University of San Francisco. Operating in Spanish, interacting with students from around the Spanish-speaking world, and building my reputation as a classically educated Latin American historian are taking my career in a new direction. Especially gratifying is designing a Great Books program that includes Spanish, Latin American, and Indigenous voices who have long spoken into the Great Conversation but have not traditionally been heard. The fully remote nature of the role means I can be present for my family. That is the most precious gift of all.

Notes

1 For a detailed discussion of Cholula's most important annual ritual, the Procession of the Lanterns, see Verónica A. Gutiérrez, "A Procession through the *Milpas*: Indigenous-Christian Ritual in Cholula, Puebla, México," Special President's Section: Celebrating the Scholarship of Women Historians in the Conference on Faith and History, *Fides et Historia* 51, no. 1 (Winter/Spring 2019): 105–23.

2 Verónica Gutiérrez, "Resilience in the Oldest City in the Americas," TEDxAzusaPacificUniversity video, filmed in Azusa, California, March 28, 2017, 13:19.

3 The professional development tour was commissioned by the Latin American Initiative of the Conference on Faith and History. The event was titled "From 1519 to 2019: Indigenous Christianity in Mexico 500 Years after Cortés" (May 28–June 3, 2019); archived tweets are available @faithandhistory #CFHMexico2019.

4 To learn more about my experience at the commemoration, see Verónica Gutiérrez, "When the Cholulteca Folded onto the Earth: Contested Commemorations of the 1519 Cholula Massacre," *Anxious Bench* (blog), Patheos, November 18, 2022, https://www.patheos.com/blogs/anxiousbench/2022/11/when-the-cholulteca-folded-onto-the-earth-contested-commemorations-of-the-1519-cholula-massacre/.

7

IGUALMENTE

Similar Struggle, Shared Success

DAMON A. HORTON

"¡Somos familia!" was a faithful word of advice deposited in my heart by my mother. Family is a pervasive cultural value for Latinas/os.[1] For many of us, *familia* extends beyond those we live with, since our love for *gente* (people) intersects us in intraethnic, interethnic, and transcultural fashions. Our lives are complex rhythms comprised of binary truths with nuanced applications as *familia*, faith, and work ground our identity. We live, learn, and love in proximity with *familia*.

The earliest depiction of the church was founded on understanding each member of the community of faith as part of a family. Joseph Hellerman asserted, "The New Testament picture of the church as a family flies in the face of our individualistic cultural orientation. God's intention is not to become the feel-good Father of many isolated individuals who appropriate the Christian faith as yet another avenue towards personal enlightenment."[2]

This chapter aims to share the story God is writing through my life as he intersects *familia*, faith, and work. Some of my experiences are unique, but my prayer is that every struggle and success will bring you affirmation, clarity, and comfort and that you will hear my heart whispering *¡Igualmente!* as a cue for you to do the same *para nuestra gente*.

Pathway to the Professoriate

I never imagined I would attend college, earn a PhD, or become a professor. Higher education was not a viable option for many inside the community I was born and raised in.[3] No one in my family went to college. Our family legacy was only grounded in hard manual and migrant labor. My great-grandparents on our Camacho and Conchola sides migrated north to the United States from México, picking crops and working in fields. After a generation, manual labor, some military ventures, and hustling in the streets were careers providing for our family. At the age of twenty, I felt I had achieved upward social mobility, since I was doing better than my dad, who worked as an overnight security guard, and my mom, who worked for over a decade at McDonald's and Walmart.

I never took the ACT or SAT exams, not even the practice exams, since college was not an option, so I thought I would never see one—until a conversation with someone who saw the potential inside of me. Standing amid a crowd holding up various items pulled out from their backpacks and pockets, my concentration broke when I noticed a smiling African American woman making her way toward the cipher circle,[4] asking direct questions like, "What are you doing with your life, Damon?" "Can you imagine the doors God would open for you if you earned a college degree?" and "Will you come by my office tomorrow to hear about a scholarship opportunity that will help you earn a college degree?"

When I walked through the doors of Donnelly College the following day, a smiling Bernetta McKindra welcomed me before expressing her gratitude for me taking her up on the previous night's offer to talk. The irony of the journey I was about to start is this: Donnelly College was a few blocks' walk from the house I lived in from when my parents brought me home from Bethany Hospital until I got married, yet, culturally, it was a world away and out of my grasp for two decades.

That meeting in December 2000 began a journey leading to earning a BS in biblical studies (2007), an MS in Christian studies (2009), and a PhD in applied theology (2022). In the Lord's design, I began serving my alma mater at Calvary University as an adjunct professor of urban studies once I earned my master's degree. In August 2019, the Lord again did the unthinkable by allowing me to serve full time at California Baptist

University as the program director of the intercultural studies program and an associate professor.

As I continue walking with Jesus through life's journey, I'm currently learning how honest scholarship requires the researcher, professor, and student to bring their *whole self* to each contribution made. I use the acronym *H.U.M.A.N.* to explain what I mean by the term *whole self.* Honest scholarship puts into dialogue the perspective of the following nuances:

- *Habitat* (our social spaces)—We share how our families of origin and the culture we were raised in and around form how we address any issue working against flourishing in the home, church, community, city, nation, and world.
- *Understanding* (our intellect)—We communicate how we are disciplined in refining our social toolkit through diligence in engaging primary sources and critically processing history and the present to offer practical ways forward, leading to life in abundance, per God's design.
- *Material* (our physical bodies)—We implicitly and explicitly demonstrate in our work how Scripture informs our behaviors regarding the stewardship of needs regarding clothing, diet, employment, exercise, fair wages, hygiene, righteous sexual expression, and affordable housing for ourselves and others.
- *Affection* (our emotions)—We proclaim how we help carve healthy pathways of awareness, coping, expressing, and healing in our arenas of emotions, mental illness, stress factors, and abuse (emotional, physical, sexual, spiritual, substance, and verbal).
- *Non-Material* (our spirituality)—We are driven by a desire to recognize the God-given soul every image bearer has received and love them enough to creatively share the good news of how Jesus is the only qualified Savior who redeems men and women from every ethnicity, class, and first language.[5]

This chapter demonstrates how I pour out my *whole self* while sharing my process of navigating as an *Evangélico*[6] serving in higher education through teaching, research, mentoring, and service. I am humbled to be one Latino voice attempting to harmonize with existing voices who paved the way for us to join in concert with their work. I aim to inspire *mi gente* to participate in our chorus.

Navigating Teaching

I did not have a non-American Latina/o scholar for required reading until one of my last PhD seminars. I will never forget the night I sat in my hotel room alone, reading the words of Ruth Padilla DeBorst masterfully explaining *Misión Integral* as mixed emotions waged war in my soul. Joy initially consumed my being because I felt like I was being shepherded by a legacy of *familia* who were using similar language to mine, not during 2020, but instead since the 1960s. Anger, in the form of sincere questions, rose from within. Questions like "Why did it take so long for me to have required reading from a Latina/o?" and "How could I have navigated in Christian higher education for over a decade and never have heard of *Misión Integral*?"

Experiences like this shaped my approach to teaching. My syllabi include the work of men and women scholars from various disciplines and Western and majority-world cultures. My pedagogical approach in the classroom results from an intentional weaving of Western and majority-world modalities, since students from both frameworks are present in the classroom. Themes such as individualism and collectivism, justice/guilt and honor/shame, and creation/redemption tie the course material together to allow students to develop a global awareness coupled with local application.

Bringing my whole self to every class gathering is ensured as I shape each session within my "Four Ts" framework. First, *truth* must be central in each lesson. I develop each class with the same hermeneutical approach for a sermon. The science portion is accomplished through exegetical work in Scripture, the content from the assigned reading, and parallel scholarly voices on themes covered in the lesson. The art portion begins with a prayer for God to fill my heart with creativity so that my imagination will consider aesthetics to help students audibly and visually process the truth I share.

Second, *transparency* is a necessary vehicle for communicating truth. I open my life before my students, like what Paul shared in 1 Thessalonians 2:8 regarding his whole life and the gospel being shared in concert. When I share the real stories of my life to illustrate a genuine concept, my students have admitted to having greater content-retention levels because the memorable story is partnered with the truth.

Third, I work to discipline my vocal *tone* so it accentuates the concept of truth I'm sharing. In moments of sincerity, I speak softly and tenderly compared to prophetic truth-telling, where my tone is informative.

Fourth, *timeliness* sets the pace of learning. When building my lesson plans, I consider different content delivery methods and when a transition from lecturing is best. I pose a few questions for small group discussion, create silent reading and reflection space, and present an open-ended question to the entire class for impromptu dialogue. When we transition back to the lecture, the concept of truth, which is essential and weighty, is presented to refreshed brains ready to interact with new content.

At the end of each semester, I analyze the feedback given by students on course evaluations. I compare that data set with another set collected from an assignment titled "Personal Reflection Survey," where I ask students direct questions on how to improve this course in the areas of textbook selection, content delivery, and topics to be covered. On the first day of class, I tell my students I am here to serve them, not the other way around. Analyzing this data and making changes that benefit the students by giving them a higher probability of achieving all the course's learning outcomes is my way of keeping my promise to them.

Navigating Research

Mi gente hold a special place in my heart that fuels my academic drive toward finding ways of encouraging Latinas/os to enter higher education and flourish throughout their journey to degree attainment. The Latina/o prospective pool for higher education is not yet near the capacity it could be due to what George Orfield et al. identify as "double segregation."[7] In the United States in 2014, 17.9 million (one-third) Latinas/os were under eighteen, and 14.6 million were millennials (aged 18–34 in 2014). Ortiz, Valerio, and Lopez reported that Latina/o enrollment in grades K–12 is the fastest growing (by 20 percent), while White enrollment decreased by 11 percent.[8] Pew Research identified the rising Latina/o birthrate inside the United States, not immigration, has contributed to this escalated growth in K–12 enrollment.[9] Schools are recruiting in regions densely populated with Latinas/os, no matter the geographic distance from their campus. The University of New Hampshire understands that recruiting Latina/o students begins during their early years of education. Sponsoring programs such as Upward Bound have proven to be successful in helping Latina/o students transition from high school to college.[10]

Though the population of Latina/o students has increased, the American academic system they are determined to advance in was built without them and other students of color in mind.[11] This system is where individual hard work only sometimes guarantees the same outcomes for all students.[12] Gloria Ladson-Billings defines the epistemology dominant in American higher education as "a system of knowledge that has both internal logic and external validity"; yet the "hegemony of the dominant paradigm . . . claims to be the only legitimate way to view the world."[13] Students of color navigating such a system often operate with the double consciousness framed by W. E. B. Du Bois,[14] or in the case of Latinas, what Anzaldúa aptly identifies as the "Mestiza Consciousness."[15] Crisp, Taggart, and Nora classify the psychosocial nuances aforementioned as "cultural mismatches" that the Latina/o students typically endure throughout K–12 and experience in higher education as well, thus contributing to academic difficulties.[16]

A developing remedy addressing these challenges is the Community Cultural Wealth model (CCW model) introduced by Dr. Tara Yosso. Dr. Yosso targeted the experiences of marginalized students of color and established the CCW model to create a new paradigm revealing their legitimate accumulated assets and resources. As differing denominations of capital emerged from Yosso's research on Latinas/os in various academic levels of learning, she identified six forms of capital that interact and overlap with one another to comprise the CCW model.[17] These forms of capital are aspirational, navigational, social, linguistic, familial, and resistant.

While applying the CCW model in a qualitative study of Latinas, Dr. Lindsay Pérez Huber astutely observed the theme of spiritual capital surfacing. She defines spiritual capital as "a set of resources and skills rooted in a spiritual connection to a reality greater than oneself. Spiritual capital can encompass religious, indigenous, and ancestral beliefs and practices learned from one's family, community, and inner self. Thus, spirituality in its many forms can provide a sense of hope and faith."[18] Intersecting her research of Latinas with spirituality, Dolores Delgado Bernal finds that "for these women, their spirituality was connected to their commitment to their families and communities. They saw their educational journey as a collaborative journey, not an individualistic one in which they were only interested in 'making money' when they graduated. Although often in conflict with their home religion, their spiritual practices inspired them and offered ways to take care of themselves."[19]

Spirituality is increasingly showing up in qualitative interviews. Scholars such as Ruth Galván are vocalizing the need for its inclusion in education: "Good pedagogy, like everyday living, consists of making present our entire lives . . . to understand and know individuals as spiritual beings, who rely on particular sources—knowledge, dreams, intuition—to struggle with life's lessons and live happy and creative lives, is to understand people holistically in all their conditions."[20]

I have shared a demonstration of tilling the fallow ground of the same academy that has attempted to systemically parse God, the first educator, out of the same field he created. Yet as Paul reminds us in 1 Corinthians 1:20 and 27, asserting, "Where is the one who is wise? Where is the scribe? Where is the debater of this age? Has not God made foolish the wisdom of the world?" and "But God chose what is foolish in the world to shame the wise; God chose what is weak in the world to shame the strong" (ESV).

I interpret the scholarship of the experts above as a welcome mat for me to provide contributions of empirical inquiry, social diagnosis, and the building of Kingdom-centric pathways for all in the academy and classrooms I teach, in addition to the global Body of Christ. As an *Evangélico* missiologist,[21] I have the dual privilege and responsibility of regularly submitting my whole self to the Lord (cf. Rom. 12) and seeking his guidance in using the creative imagination he's supplied me with to identify methods of evangelism and discipleship in each arena he's opened the door for me to walk in. In my research, spiritual capital is proving to be a model I leverage for my research and my approach to mentorship and service to my university.

Navigating Mentoring

My theological praxis of discipleship and mentoring operate within the framework of *Misión Integral*. According to C. René Padilla, *Misión Integral* is committed to the following convictions:

1. The commitment to Jesus Christ being Lord of everything and everyone. Padilla says, "The integral church is one which recognizes that all the spheres of life are 'mission fields' and looks for ways of asserting the sovereignty of Jesus Christ in all of them."
2. Discipleship is a progressive transformation lasting a lifetime and extending to every aspect of life.
3. The church is the community confessing Jesus Christ is truly Lord of everything and everyone. Those living out are witnesses of Christ's inauguration of a new humanity.
4. Gifts and ministries are the means used by the Spirit of God to equip the church as an agent of change in society—a change that reflects God's plan for human life and the whole creation—and to equip all the faithful for the fulfillment of their vocation as God's coworkers in the world. Every regenerate member in the church equally shares the burden of evangelizing the lost, seeking moral purity, and meeting the needs of the afflicted in harmony with James 1:27.[22]

Within this framework, I reshape the forms of capital in the CCW model to form six spokes connected to one hub. I draft a mentoring map centering spiritual capital (the hub) to ground the six forms of capital. During the semester, I regularly meet with a select few students who have asked for mentorship and apply discipleship, informing their *whole selves.*

In Ephesians 1:3–6, Paul tells Christians they have been blessed with "every spiritual blessing in the heavenly places," which identifies a spiritual treasury of benefits God the Father gives. These blessings are not found in Christians of color alone. Instead, the entire *multicultural, multiethnic, multigenerational,* and *multilinguistic* Body of Christ (Rev. 7:9). Every Jesus follower has a never-ending supply of spiritual capital, so when we choose to distribute it through the other six forms of capital, we can naturally engage evangelistic and discipleship activities.

- **Aspirational capital** reminds us our life is a vapor, and in humility, we should submit our dreams, hopes, and plans to the Lord (James 4:13–16).

- **Navigational capital** can intersect the unbeliever with the fact that God is the one who determines our steps (Prov. 16:9), so we should seek him holistically (Matt. 6:33).
- **Social capital** reminds us of the social and spiritual ethics of God's Kingdom Jesus preached, modeled, and called us to imitate (Matt. 5–7; 28:20).
- **Linguistic capital** calls us to pursue purity in our hearts, which is the well of words we draw from to speak (Matt. 12:34), and if we want to practice the religion that honors God, we should meet the felt needs of others while guarding our speech (James 1:27; 3:1–12).
- **Familial capital** points us to the fact that the Christian faith is a family, and over fifty "one another"s in the New Testament call us to live like we're family!
- **Resistant capital** is our clarion call to resist the lust of the flesh, the lust of the eyes, and the pride of life (1 John 2:15–17) and seek to be transformed by the renewing of our minds, so we do not live like those who do not know Christ (Rom. 12).

When believers leverage our God-given spiritual capital in ways that discover and develop all other forms of capital and filter them through the lens of Scripture, holistic discipleship can result. Meaningful relationships of mobilized saints will reduce lostness while disciples are being produced. All this forms a preview of what Revelation 21–22 projects Kingdom life will be like when we're dwelling in the glory of our God.

Navigating Service/Administration

As a program director, I'm privileged to have ample opportunities to walk alongside students while praying and processing the Lord's next steps for them. Our meeting times include prayer, listening to their heart, and helping affirm growth areas while sharing with them resources to strengthen the areas of opportunity for more significant development. Latina/o students I've had the privilege to walk with for at least a semester often share how they were drawn to schedule an appointment with or request mentorship from me and identify three consistent reasons for reaching out.

First, they felt seen when I spoke in Spanish or pronounced Spanish words correctly during class. They felt represented and encouraged by what they called a "Latino academic who didn't forget who he was and where he came from." Second, they respected how I led with transparency in my lectures, answers to questions, or takes on controversial social issues. They sensed security in knowing that if I were willing to be transparent in public, I would be the same in private, ensuring their safety when they wanted to open up about their calling, life experiences, or questions about faith. Third, since I would express biblically grounded sentiments about current social issues, they perceived I would understand their vantage point of life and help them identify blind spots or allow them space to be human and express their candid thoughts about where they are in life.

Lastly, I am getting better at protecting my calendar so that outside of my family and local church service, the university I serve at gets priority in my schedule. Serving as a member of the Racial Equity Task Force has provided me space to provide advisement alongside colleagues from a diversity of disciplines, ethnicities, research foci, and lived experiences and yet have the common confession that Jesus is our Lord in common. We have been able to help provide insight from voices often marginalized by the ears of executive administration.

Serving in these ways connects my *whole self* to the mission of California Baptist University. I'm motivated daily to receive what I can from the Lord, so I have plenty to give to those I encounter on campus. I'm not perfect in my approach to every moment of my workday. My struggles with diagnosed mental illnesses and my short-term memory loss provide me with consequences that often cause me to repeat a task, and that can exhaust my energy more rapidly than teaching four classes back-to-back every Tuesday and Thursday from 10:30 a.m. to 5:45 p.m.

Conclusion

I close with one final story as a capstone to our conversation. Recently the grief of losing my parents, my mother-in-law, and a few uncles within the past two years has drained me. There are more days that I don't want to get out of bed than average. However, I asked the Lord for grace and strength. One day last week, three students booked appointments to meet with me. The first meeting was about helping a student catch up on missing assignments. The following two appointments were back-to-back with students struggling with depression.

The meetings ended with the students encouraged and referred to our student services for connections with resources to help meet their needs. Driving home, I realized how drained I was but understood this comes with the calling, and I was grateful the Lord was able to use me to provide the students with hope. That night, things were very challenging at home, and I went to bed early, absolutely tapped out. The following day, I had no desire to teach four classes back-to-back, and I wanted to cancel all my classes to take a mental-health day. I advise my students to take one mental-health day in my class if they need margin to regroup and refresh.

I asked my wife, Elicia, to hold me accountable by checking on me for an hour to ensure I went to work. An hour later, Elicia called, and I was already on campus. I took a couple of hours before my first class to pray, read Scripture, and listen to a playlist I titled "*nephesh*," a fascinating Hebrew word that can be understood as our soul. I then opened my classes the same way as always: I prayed and then asked them "How are you doing?" to invite them to share a burden, praise report, question, or random thought to help cultivate a space of safety and transparency.

After the last comment in response to my question was shared, I took about ten minutes to share with all my students my struggle with exhaustion and that my drive to come to work, if I was genuinely able to, was to see them because of our great interactions. I took most of the time sharing how the greatest demonstration of faith and work integration I could give them was not a paper to write. It wasn't an exam, a vocabulary quiz, or a book report. The embodiment of faith and work integration would be seen best when I opened my life by sharing the depth of my struggle as a Latino husband, dad, pastor, and professor while offering a way to endure by intersecting God's Word, the spiritual discipline of reflection, and dependency on God the Holy Spirit. Sharing the nuances of the struggle and enduring through them in the sight of eyewitnesses provide the needed credibility in normalizing the seasons of success God gives us.

First Corinthians 1:3–7 reminds us God provided us comfort during our struggles, so by faith, as we endure and remain in Christ, we will reach seasons of success. Then we will serve as God's conduits of comfort for our brothers and sisters in Christ who are in the season of struggle. Our ability to walk alongside them will help guide them to a season of success, in which we will celebrate with them. They can then, in turn, do the same for another brother or sister in Christ. When we experience this repeatedly during this life, our legacy will be one of whispering *¡Igualmente!*

Notes

1   Linda Skogrand, Daniel Hatch, and Archana Singh, "Understanding Latino Families, Implications for Family Education," Utah State University Press, Family Resources, July 2005.

2   Joseph H. Hellerman, *When the Church Was a Family: Recapturing Jesus' Vision for Authentic Christian Community* (Nashville, TN: B&H Academic, 2009), 7.

3   The high school I graduated from has a Latina/o enrollment of 65.7 percent alongside an African American enrollment of 16.2 percent (totaling 81.9 percent). As a Title I school, it offers no AP courses, has a 44.2 percent chronically absent student population, and has a dropout population twice the district average and four times greater than the state average. The Civil Rights Data Collection database was accessed to find the related data. See their website at https://ocrdata.ed.gov.

4   When exegeted within the context of hip-hop culture, a cipher circle often includes a crowd of people surrounding emcees who are delivering improvised rhyme schemes using either objects or words shouted from the onlookers. It may also

include emcees who recite a previously written verse. It is noteworthy to mention a significant portion of terms used within hip-hop culture were adopted from the teachings of the Nation of Gods and Earths. According to the Supreme Mathematics, the number zero is represented by the term *cipher*. Since a cipher is a complete circle of 360 degrees, it is understood the 120 lessons, if they are known (knowledge), applied (wisdom), and overstood (understanding), then one's cipher (or being) is complete at 360 degrees. For more information, see God Supreme Allah, *Supreme Lessons of the Gods and Earths: A Guide for 5 Percenters to Follow as Taught by Clarence 13X Allah* (Plantation, FL: African American Bookstore, 1993).

5   The context of the development of H.U.M.A.N. and how it fits within the schema of ethnic conciliation can be read in Damon A. Horton, *Intensional: Kingdom Ethnicity in a Divided World* (Colorado Springs, CO: NavPress, 2019).

6   I define *Evangélico* as Latina/o Protestant Christians who are committed to proclaiming the gospel and doing the work of discipleship while applying the Scripture as the guardrails for their social activism. I ground this definition in light of the fact Evangélicos are often associated with the missiological praxis known as Misión Integral (or holistic mission). Ruth Padilla DeBorst identifies the founders of Misión Integral as Lilly and Samuel Escobar, Emma and Pedro Arana, and Caty and René Padilla Emilio. DeBorst defines Misión Integral as "a theological-missiological articulation and practice that seeks to engage followers of Jesus in linking the whole gospel to the whole of life under the lordship of Christ in the power of the Holy Spirit so that the reign of God and God's justice may be made visible in particular historical contexts." Ruth Padilla DeBorst, "Church, Power, and Transformation in Latin America: A Different Citizenship Is Possible," in *Majority World Theology: Christian Doctrine in the Global Context* (Downers Grove, IL: InterVarsity Press, 2020), 503–4. Emilio A. Núñez says, "Evangélicos are theocentric, bibliocentric, Christocentric, and pneumatological" in "Towards an Evangelical Latin American Theology," *Evangelical Review of Theology* 7, no. 1 (1983): 125–31. According to David Stoll, Evangélicos are those who "pursue social issues without abandoning evangelism, deal with the oppressive structures without endorsing violence, and bring left and right-wing Protestants back together again," as published in *Is Latin America Turning Protestant: The Politics of Evangelical Growth* (Berkeley: University of California Press, 1990), 131.

7   The term *double segregation* is used to describe how both race and poverty affect African American and Latino students, whose K–12 enrollment in schools seldom sees successful outcomes when compared to middle-class schools with populations dominated by White and Asian student demographics. George Orfield et al., "Brown at 62: School Segregation by Race, Poverty, and State," Civil Rights Project / Proyecto Derechos Civiles UCLA, 2016, https://www.civilrightsproject.ucla.edu/research/k-12-education/integration-and-diversity/brown-at-62-school-segregation-by-race-poverty-and-state/.

8 Carlos J. Ortiz, Melissa A. Valerio, and Kristina Lopez, "Trends in Hispanic Academic Achievement," *Journal of Hispanic Higher Education* 11, no. 2 (2012): 136–48.

9 Jens Manuel Krogstad, Jeffrey S. Passel, and Luis Noe-Bustamante, "Key Facts about U.S. Latinos for National Hispanic Heritage Month," Pew Research, September 23, 2022.

10 Kimberly Greenwood, "Higher Education Marketing to the Hispanic Student Population," honors thesis, University of New Hampshire, Spring 2012, http://scholars.unh.edu/cgi/viewcontent.cgi?article=1049&context=honors.

11 In 1975, Jennifer Hurstfield drew on Robert Blauner's *Racial Oppression in America* (New York: Harper & Row, 1972) to evaluate the educational experiences of Blacks, Chicanos (Mexican Americans), and Indigenous Americans. Blauner argued the educational experiences of said ethnicities are to be interpreted through the lens of colonization based on the following five colonial relationships: colonized groups are forced to be a part of the dominant society through conquest and enslavement; the colonized are placed in categories of low status; the colonized are subject to White bureaucratic control in every area of life; the culture of the colonized is transformed, depreciated, or destroyed; and the colonized are victims of racism, which rationalizes White dominance over them. Hurstfield centered her study on the southwestern portion of the United States during a time when this was the geographic nucleus of her target population. Her findings support Blauner's framework with data demonstrating how the depreciation of the Chicano culture and language "condemned them to low achievement and inhibited Chicano parents from playing a more effective role in the educational process." Valencia and Solórzano see this cultural deficit approach as "rooted in models of cultural and biological determinism" regarding "social science and history," resulting in a distortion of "Chicana/o experiences" and "'see[ing]' only deprivation in Communities of Color." Richard R. Valencia and Daniel Solórzano, "Contemporary Deficit Thinking," in *The Evolution of Deficit Thinking in Educational Thought and Practice* (New York: Falmer, 1997), 160–210. Conceptually, the cultural deficit model gained popularity in the late 1950s. The research focused on assessing the education of children from the lower social class of America and Black children in the same social category. According to Bernstein, those who fit the above demographic were labeled culturally deprived, inferring that the parents of these students were inadequate, as were their culture, images, and symbols. Bernstein adds, "The child is expected, and his parents as well, to drop their social identity, their way of life and its symbolic representation, at the school gate. For, by definition, their culture is deprived, the parents inadequate in both the moral and skill orders they transmit." Basil Bernstein, *Class, Codes, and Control*, vol. 1, *Theoretical Studies towards a Sociology of Language* (New York: Routledge, 2003), 148–49.

12 Dolores Delgado Bernal and Octavio Villalpando, "An Apartheid of Knowledge in Academia: The Struggle over the 'Legitimate' Knowledge of Faculty of Color," in *Foundations of Critical Race Theory in Education*, 2nd ed., ed. Edward Taylor, David Gillborn, and Gloria Ladson-Billings (New York: Routledge, 2016), 80. In her

article "Unequal Opportunity: Race and Education" (Brookings, March 1, 1998, https://www.brookings.edu/articles/unequal-opportunity-race-and-education/), Linda Darling-Hammond asserts economics play a key role in educational disparity. In communities where ethnic minority students are the dominant population as well as rural communities where White students are dominant, both suffer from economic oppression that reduces the amount of educational funding and instructional resources from their state government. A more recent report—Nathan Joo, Richard V. Reeves, and Edward Rodrigue's "Asian-American Success and the Pitfalls of Generalization," Brookings, April 20, 2016, https://www.brookings.edu/research/asian-american-success-and-the-pitfalls-of-generalization/—argues Far East Asian students in America are successful inside the American educational sphere; however, students from Southeast Asia (specifically Cambodia and Hmong ethnicities) are underperforming. The dividing line used to determine success and underperformance is the academic scores of White students. The data revealed the Southeast Asian students live in economically oppressed communities and attend schools that lack funding and instructional resources.

13 Gloria Ladson-Billings, "Racialized Discourses and Ethnic Epistemologies," in *Handbook of Qualitative Research*, 2nd ed., ed. Norman K. Denzin and Yvonna S. Lincoln (Thousand Oaks, CA: Sage, 2000), 257–77.

14 In *The Souls of Black Folk*, Du Bois identifies double consciousness as "this sense of always looking at one's self through the eyes of others, of measuring one's soul by the tape of a world that looks on in amused contempt and pity." W. E. B. Du Bois, *The Souls of Black Folk* (New York: Dover, 1903), 2–3.

15 Anzaldúa defines mestiza consciousness as the "dual or multiple personality" that's plagued by "psychic restlessness," yet within *la cultura chicana*, commonly held beliefs of White culture attack the Mexican culture, and both attack the Indigenous culture. What's necessary is the addition of the (whole) self, which shapes the mestiza consciousness that flows as a source of "energy [that] comes from continual creative motion that keeps breaking down the unitary aspect of each new paradigm." Gloria Anzaldúa, *Borderlands / La Frontera*, 2nd ed. (San Francisco: Aunt Lute Books, 1999), 100–103.

16 Gloria Crisp, Amanda Taggart, and Amaury Nora, "Undergraduate Latina/o Students: A Systematic Review of Research Identifying Factors Contributing to Academic Success Outcomes," *RER* 85 (2015): 249–74.

17 The various levels meaning elementary, middle, high, and postsecondary school (including graduate and doctoral work).

18 Lindsay Pérez Huber, "Challenging Racist Nativist Framing: Acknowledging the Community Cultural Wealth of Undocumented Chicana College Students to Reframe the Immigration Debate," *HER* 79 (2009): 721.

19 Dolores Delgado Bernal, "Learning and Living Pedagogies of the Home: The Mestiza Consciousness of Chicana Students," *International Journal of Qualitative Studies in Education* 14, no. 5 (2001): 635.

20 Ruth Trinidad Galván, "*Campesina* Epistemologies and Pedagogies of the Spirit: Examining Women's *Sobrevivencia*," in *Chicana/Latina Education in Everyday Life: Feminista Perspectives on Pedagogy and Epistemology*, ed. Dolores Delgado Bernal and C. Alejandra Elenes (Albany: State University of New York Press, 2006), 161–79.

21 My calling and credentials warrant the discipline of missiology being identified as my vocation. I define missiology as *an independent academic tradition that draws upon disciplines such as anthropology, ethnic studies, history, philosophy, psychology, religious studies, sociology, and theology to assess how the Christian Church has and should engage in missions*. This definition is grounded in answering the question "Is missiology an academic discipline?" Jan A. B. Jongeneel says, "Yes; because it involves both methodological distance to—Christian and non-Christian—mission (cf. the philosophy of mission and the science of mission) and methodological commitment or 'engagement' to—Christian—mission (cf. the theology of mission, missionary theology)." See his "Is Missiology an Academic Discipline?," *Transformation* 15, no. 3 (1998): 31. Alan R. Tippet defines missiology as "the academic discipline or science which researches, records, and applies data relating to the biblical origin, the history (including the use of documentary materials), the anthropological principles and techniques and the theology base of Christian mission" in *Introduction to Missiology* (Pasadena, CA: William Cary Library, 1987), xiii. John Mark Terry says missiology is not static, and although it draws heavily on theology and history, it must also engage "the behavioral sciences, namely, anthropology, sociology, psychology, and linguistics" in *Missiology: An Introduction to the Foundations, History, and Strategies of World Missions* (Nashville, TN: B&H Publishing, 2015), 8.

22 C. René Padilla, *The Local Church, Agent of Transformation: An Ecclesiology for Integral Mission* (Buenos Aires: Ediciones Kairós, 2004), 28–43.

8

A DIFFICULT JOURNEY

From First-Generation Student
to Two-Time President and Trustee

Pete C. Menjares

Nothing I have done in my life or career has been easy, and there have been times when the work I was called to do was outright impossible and not in the least enjoyable. Yet I am one of the fortunate ones to have enjoyed a successful three-decades-long career in Christian higher education as a professor, administrator, two-time president, and trustee. Further, I am a graduate of a Christian university, my wife and daughter got their degrees from a Christian university, and we are donors. As a member of the faculty, I was successfully promoted, tenured, and honored by my faculty colleagues with the highest award given to a member of the faculty. As an administrator, I was fortunate to lead a successful and growing department and launch a new administrative unit that would advance the university's understanding of race and faith in new and important ways. As a provost, I was part of the academic and administrative teams leading the university through the COVID-19 pandemic and successfully transitioned an institution from primarily seated instruction to remote leading. Following a national search, I would become the eleventh president of a four-year liberal arts university in my home state of California. As a member of the board of trustees of a midsize national university, I was in the position to provide presidential leadership in a time of crisis and transition in senior leadership. I am also

Latino, a third-generation, English-dominant Mexican American born and raised in the city of Los Angeles in the Lincoln Heights and Boyle Heights communities.

As the first person in my family to go to college, I never imagined graduating with a university degree, let alone being a university professor. I had no mental schema for this, no role models to emulate, and the men in my hardworking Mexican American family typically went into the military or work after graduating from high school. Before my own college graduation, I had never even been to a commencement ceremony, nor did I know any college graduates growing up other than my elementary and secondary school teachers and parish priest who attended seminary. No college students or university graduates were sitting around our dinner table discussing mathematics, literature, art, philosophy, or the social sciences, let alone the emerging fields of ethnic and cultural studies. I never saw anyone reading a book or modeling the disciplines needed to learn a subject or earn good grades. For that matter, I never saw anyone read a book for the sheer joy that reading gives or the love of learning. These experiences were necessary to gain the requisite skills to do well at any level of my formal education. No wonder I had to receive supplemental instruction, basic skills tutoring, and summer school to be promoted to the next grade. It is no wonder that I graduated from high school only because of the help I got from taking special classes under the supervision of a few caring teachers. Therefore, it is not surprising that I struggled and dropped out in my first year when I attempted to take classes at the local community college after high school. That was a painful experience that would follow me my entire educational career as my first official college transcript was marked with the words SCHOLASTIC PROBATION.

My father was tragically killed at the age of twenty-three. I was only months old when this happened, and my twenty-year-old mother was pregnant with my sister. My mother would eventually remarry and then divorce before I could start my first grade in elementary school. She would move us out of the Lincoln Heights neighborhood where my father was killed and soon relocate us to the community of Pico Rivera, about ten miles west of Los Angeles. Being raised by a single mom, my younger siblings and I attended public school and went to catechism on Saturday mornings at our local Catholic church. I would be confirmed in the Roman Catholic Church and eventually attend a college prep Catholic high school. However, my faith was nominal at best, and I continued to struggle in school, not for lack of intelligence but for lack of interest and an inability to wisely manage my time and the distractions of youth. All this would change after high school when I would have a life-transforming encounter with Jesus Christ as he was being boldly preached on the streets of East Los Angeles at a time now known as the Jesus Movement. My new relationship with Christ ignited a desire to read and learn the Scriptures. In this quest, I would discover the book of Proverbs and the verse that would profoundly impact my life and subsequent calling to teach:

> The fear of the Lord is the beginning of wisdom,
> And the knowledge of the Holy One is insight. (Prov. 9:10 ESV)

Following a short stint stocking a furniture warehouse and later working for a telephone company, I would eventually reenroll at the community college, mindful not to repeat the failures of my first attempt and to begin the pathway to the professoriate slowly.

I would eventually transfer and become a religion major at Southern California College (now Vanguard University), a small Christian college in Costa Mesa, California, known for its stellar and caring faculty, excellence in teaching, and track record for preparing women and men for ministry in the local church and on the mission field. I was inspired to learn by my professors, who were passionate about their subjects, took a personal interest in us as students and individuals, and took their calling to teach seriously. Their enthusiasm for teaching and mentoring was infectious. Before too long, I began to imagine myself as a classroom professor someday teaching Bible or theology at the same college or other theological seminaries. However, to do so meant that I would have to attend graduate school. That objective also appeared impossible due to the number of obstacles I would have to overcome. Yet God's providence would lead faculty, pastors, and leaders in my church to journey with me, believe in me, and encourage me to pursue my dreams. Friends and classmates also committed to journeying together toward whatever God was calling us to, including graduate education. Each of these individuals played a part in my goal to achieve a college degree in addition to God's miraculous provision of scholarships, grants, tuition discounts, and a doctoral fellowship. Without significant financial assistance, I would not have attended accredited institutions or finished my studies in a timely manner.

My faith journey profoundly influenced my pathway to the professoriate, family upbringing, geographical location, and educational experiences—K–12, public, and Catholic, including my initial failure in community college. My family circumstances sensitized me to the realities of fatherlessness, the number of families being led by single moms, and the fragility of human relationships; the city of my birth, Los Angeles, is characterized by cultural, ethnic, religious, and economic diversity, yet racial tensions and class divisions persist to this day; and working on my doctoral degree at the University of Southern California (USC) while also teaching public middle school in one of the most impoverished communities in the city during the 1992 riots lit a fire in me to advocate for more equitable educational opportunities for the urban poor. The accumulation of my life experiences, the aftermath of significant social events, and a renewed commitment to educational advocacy, equity, and justice converged at the time just before my being invited to teach at Biola University. This convergence would help clarify my core values, shape my identity, and impact my teaching, scholarship, mentoring, and service in new and profound ways.

Navigating Teaching

I came into teaching at a time when my Latino peers and I were the first Hispanics in our departments, schools, academic divisions, and even our colleges or universities. Being the first of your kind, whether female or male, Black, Asian, Hispanic, or other, carried a weight of responsibility that our majority-culture colleagues did not have to bear. Navigating negative stereotypes was a daily occurrence, being looked to as the representative and voice of an entire people group was frustrating, and once Latino students and other students of color discovered you were on campus, they sought you out for advice, mentoring, and safety. The invisible burdens we bore in those early years were real. They were exhausting, especially since you were still expected to be excellent in the classroom, available during office hours for students, prepared for department meetings, responsible in your committee work, willingly taking on all other duties as assigned, and successfully working toward promotion and tenure, if you were fortunate enough to be on the tenure track, and I was.

Further, early career faculty were not paid much, and in informal comparisons of salaries with colleagues at public universities, I seemed to be making far less than they were. And for those early career faculty with families like mine, the relatively low pay led to teaching overloads and taking on additional assignments for the extra pay. These invisible burdens eventually take their toll and can lead to anger and resentment, discouragement, burnout, and an eventual leaving the university or teaching altogether, which was the case for some of my peers of color and women colleagues. How was I able to successfully navigate the early stages of teaching and the invisible baggage associated with being the first Latino PhD in my department and one of only a handful of Latino faculty members in a Christian university less than twenty miles from the city of Los Angeles, in a county that was nearly 60 percent Latino?

To begin, I knew what I was getting into from the start. For instance, I was first approached to teach at Biola University by a friend of mine who worked there, and he was explicit about the fact that the department needed someone with my background and experience—namely, a Latino with professional preparation in the field of education and with a solid Christian faith. I had both. My colleague also had insight into the internal workings of the university that would ultimately assist me with navigating the culture and environment once I started. The other factor that helped prepare me for the journey came from the department chair who hired me. Dr. Lucille Richardson was a former principal at a large public high school in diverse Los Angeles County. She was aware of the realities of urban youth and the kinds of teachers needed to help them succeed in the classroom and in life. She was also aware of the challenges of being a female African American administrator at a predominantly White Christian university in the early 1990s. I had instant respect for her as a person, for her professional credentials, and for her candor on what it was like to be a racial minority in that space. She understood the context, and she understood me. To this day, I vividly recall her words in the interview when she said, "You are one of a handful of Latino males with a PhD from an R1 urban research university, and you will have lots of universities lining up to hire you. And I understand that you don't need us, but we need you.

Come and be a missionary to us. Come and teach us about the city and multiculturalism so we are ready when it happens here."

The final piece that prepared me early was a clear and unmistakable sense of calling to teach there. Although my department chair was complimentary and confident that I would have lines of universities offering me a teaching position, I did not. I did, however, have one offer to teach, and I had agreed to return a signed teaching contract to the dean of education at a local California state university on the same day I interviewed at Biola. Having concluded my Biola interview and recalling the words "You don't need us, but we need you. Come and be a missionary to us . . ." something profound happened in me, and my spirit began to stir as I walked across the small suburban campus. At that time, I had been away from Christian higher education and service in a faith-based organization for over five years while I attended graduate school and prepared for a career in educational research. The last thing I expected on that late summer day was an encounter with the Holy Spirit and the conviction that I was being called to teach at a Christian university and serve in God's Kingdom. The conviction of the Holy Spirit was so strong and the calling to teach so clear that I began to cry as I walked to my car. As I drove to the state university, I could not stop crying, shake my feeling, or ignore what was happening to me. And as further evidence of my divine encounter, when I got to the door of the dean's office to leave my contract, I discovered a note that said the dean was out but would return shortly. It was at that moment that I realized I was not to take the state university teaching position, and I wrote a short note of explanation to the dean about why I could not accept the offer. In retrospect, that was a bold act of faith, because Biola had yet to offer me a teaching position, yet the conviction that God was leading me to Kingdom service gave me the peace to know that I was being called to something greater than I had imagined. Not long after that, Biola would offer me a position to teach, thus confirming what the Holy Spirit put in my heart weeks earlier regarding the call to teach and provide Christian service. The significance of this encounter with the Holy Spirit would continue to unfold over the course of my early teaching career and subsequently redirect my research agenda while opening the door to academic administration and service to the broader Christian higher education community.

In retrospect, knowing that I had the educational preparation and life experiences the department needed, understanding that I would have to navigate an institutional culture and racial climate that were unlike those of the diverse urban universities where I received my graduate education, realizing from the start that my "missionary" assignment would encompass the classroom and the spaces beyond the classroom, and having a clear sense of calling to teach and a Kingdom mindset were foundational to my early success. I would ultimately go on to develop and teach various courses in undergraduate and graduate education, oversee clinical placements, teach capstone courses, oversee capstone research, and serve on doctoral dissertation committees at various academic schools and institutions. I would further contribute to developing numerous co-curricular projects and experiential learning experiences in the city. My teaching efforts would earn the respect of my faculty peers and leadership, allow me to be successfully promoted and awarded tenure, and ultimately lead to my being given the Robert B. Fischer Award for Faculty Excellence, the highest faculty award voted upon by the faculty. The award recognizes individual faculty for outstanding contributions to the university through quality teaching, engaging scholarship, committed service, and student mentoring. I was humbled to receive the award and honored to be numbered with the previous winners because I never entered the professoriate to win awards or achieve accolades; I wanted to be faithful to my call to teach and provide Kingdom service.

Navigating Research

I had as close to the ideal graduate education as one could hope. At both the master's and doctoral levels, I did well in my coursework and was close to my professors. My master's-level work was a combined academic degree and professional preparation program, since I was also working on my secondary education Professional Clear Credential in English language arts. I was teaching middle school English at the time on an emergency permit, so it was imperative that I complete the coursework needed for the Clear Credential. I expected to take courses in educational foundations, secondary methods, and other required subjects for the credential. Still, in getting to know my professors and their work beyond the classroom, I was fortunate to discover a world unbeknown to me at the time: the world of educational research. It didn't take long for me to realize that several professors were conducting original research, writing papers, and making presentations at professional conferences. Several had received grants to fund their research projects and even employed students as research assistants. Near the end of my master's-level work, I was invited to serve on a project by assisting my professor with bibliographic research to review the literature she was preparing for publication. That was my first taste of educational research, and I loved it. Seeing my enthusiasm and capacity for research, my professor and other faculty in the division encouraged me to pursue a doctoral degree and to focus on earning a PhD so I would be equipped with the tools to conduct independent research. After a period of discernment, prayer, and review of several PhD programs in the region, including campus visits and interviews with program directors, I was providentially led to USC, where I began my doctoral studies in the spring of 1993.

I mentioned that I was providentially led because, due to a series of life circumstances out of my control, I could not enroll in a PhD program the fall term after graduating with my master of arts degree. I was still not convinced about where to study. At a Thanksgiving dinner for family and friends hosted at our home, I spoke with one of my wife's cousins, who asked what I planned to do now that I was done with my master's. I mentioned that I had planned to enroll in a doctoral program as soon as I could find the right fit for me and my interests. It was at that moment that she reminded me that she was employed in a key staff position in the School of Education at USC, and if I was interested, she would take it upon herself to arrange a meeting with me and the dean of the school and any of the program directors I wanted to meet. I didn't hesitate to take her up on the invitation, and within a week, I was at her office ready for my tour, and she was true to her word. Over the course of my tour, I met the school dean, several key staff who would prove critical to my success in navigating paperwork and procedures, and the program director who would ultimately become my mentor and doctoral dissertation chair. Dr. Robert Rueda was generous with his time from the moment I met him, and he spent over an hour answering my questions and encouraging me in my pursuit of the PhD. Like me, he was also a Latino raised in a Roman Catholic family and the product of Catholic schools on the east side of Los Angeles. Dr. Rueda also respected my wife's cousin Brenda and promised to be on the lookout for me if I enrolled in his program.

I would indeed enroll and begin coursework in the PhD program at USC under the mentorship of Dr. Rueda, who challenged me intellectually and held me to very high standards in the classroom and soon as his research assistant. He would be instrumental in my achieving a doctoral fellowship that would pay for my tuition and provide a stipend for educational expenses as well as hire me to assist him with several research projects. I would learn every aspect of research from him, from completing the research proposal to budget management, adhering to compliance regulations, filing the proper paperwork in a timely manner, writing the research report, presenting research findings at professional conferences, and coauthoring publications. It was an ideal education and preparation for what God would call me to do in Christian higher education. However, in our last meeting after graduation, he gave me a word of advice that has stayed with me since. He said that I would be one of a handful of Latino PhDs with a degree from an R1 institution and that there would be universities lining up to hire me, and his last word to me was, "Don't be seduced by the attention." I would take these words to heart and commit to being on guard against pride and cultivating humility in my life and work.

It was gratifying to complete my doctoral work, successfully defend my dissertation, and publish my first journal article. Several of my fellow doctoral classmates were also publishing their studies and taking teaching positions at various universities. As I reflected on my journey to that point, I became increasingly aware of how privileged I was to achieve the highest academic degree in my field and embark on the next phase of my career. I also came across the words of the preacher in the book of Ecclesiastes,

> I have seen something else under the sun:
> The race is not to the swift
> or the battle to the strong,
> nor does food come to the wise
> or wealth to the brilliant
> or favor to the learned;
> but time and chance happen to them all.

(Eccl. 9:11 NIV)

This verse recalled the quote of the famous French scientist and micro-biologist Louis Pasteur, who said, "Chance favors the prepared mind." I had never been the fastest, strongest, wisest, most brilliant, or most learned of my peers, but I had been the beneficiary of time and chance, and I can only credit God for the life he gave me and the education made possible by his grace. My life experiences and professional training would prepare me for the moment the Biola administration needed someone to conduct the first comprehensive campus climate study at a critical point in its racial history. The findings would lead to significant structural and cultural changes at the institution. This same preparation would enable me to take the methods and outcomes of the campus climate study to a national audience by way of the Council for Christian Colleges and Universities (CCCU) at a critical time in its racial history. Was this the plan following my graduation from USC? Not at all. I intended to establish myself as an educational researcher focused on studying Latino students' higher education access and achievement, establish a research center, subsidize the center with grant funding, conduct research, present my findings at national conferences, and write many books. However, God would have other plans for my research, which would consider the needs of Latino students and students from various ethnic backgrounds that happened to be enrolled in Christian colleges, universities, and seminaries across the CCCU. What I also didn't realize at that time was God's will for me in administration and service, first to Biola and then to other institutions.

Navigating Mentoring

I have been fortunate to have had Latino women and men in my life to provide guidance and encouragement on the journey to the professoriate and to serve as role models for navigating the various twists and turns that marked the stages in my career. I have benefited from the wisdom, insights, and experiences of others who were generous with their time and patience with me as I sought to apply what they imparted to my unique context and circumstances. For instance, as a young man, I profoundly benefited from the entire pastoral staff of my small Assemblies of God church, since they all had college degrees and expected me to have one too. Reverend James Ortiz mentored me in the faith and gave me my start in local church ministry. When it was time for me to receive formal training, he ensured that I enrolled at his alma mater, Southern California College, so that I would be spiritually and professionally prepared. Dr. Jose Arreguín, professor and cofounder of the Hispanic Ministries Center at Fuller Theological Seminary, showed me what it was like to be an educated Latino who was both a person of faith and a professor and how to integrate my faith, identity, and calling. Dr. Jesse Miranda modeled educational leadership, national ministry, courage, and civic engagement. Dr. Robert Rueda held me to the highest academic standards and modeled professional integrity and generosity of time and resources. These key individuals are only a handful of the mentors from whom I have benefited and whose influence made me the person I am today.

Jesus said, "Freely you have received; freely give" (Matt. 10:8 NIV). Being the recipient of such a rich mentoring legacy comes with the responsibility to pass on what I have learned, known, and experienced to others. My desire to teach and tendency toward generosity have naturally oriented me toward mentoring. As I transition to a new season in life and career, my commitment to doing so has been strengthened. There is also a tremendous need to mentor the next generation of Latinos entering the professoriate and those moving up the ranks. Though there may be more Latinos earning doctorates and embarking on careers in academia, many of the same conditions that characterized my generation persist, as evidenced in the lives of those Latino professionals I currently mentor. In many instances, they continue to be underrepresented in their fields, encounter negative stereotypes from those they report to and lead, work at balancing their career aspirations with raising young families, and remain intentional about maintaining their physical health and overall well-being. Emerging Latino professors still need to be nurtured, encouraged, and recognized for the gifts they bring to the academy. They need those of us who are more professionally established to help open doors of opportunity for them, create space, make room, and empower them to pursue their dreams and aspirations boldly. They need mentors in teaching, research, writing, publishing, speaking, and service at each stage of their careers from nailing their first interview to successfully navigating the tenure process. They also need to hear the stories of those who have gone before them and to know they are a part of a legacy of Latino educators of faith who were courageous, persistent, and dignified.

Navigating Service/Administration

I had only been in the education department for less than a year when my department chair, Dr. Lucille Richardson, was called to the mission field. I was genuinely excited for Lucille and the new ministry opportunity before her. I assumed the vacated chair position would go to one of my more established and experienced colleagues. One can imagine my surprise when the dean of the school and others in upper administration approached me to consider taking the chair role. I was incredulous at the invitation for several reasons. For one, I had only been in the department for a short time, and second, I had never been in a chair role before. Third, I was still finishing my doctoral work and needed to defend my dissertation successfully. And finally, I was earning a PhD because I wanted to teach, conduct research, and write without being bogged down with administrative minutia. Yet something was intriguing about the opportunity to provide departmental leadership at a critical time for teacher education in the region and state. Academic oversight was not completely foreign to me, since I had been a full-time administrative pastor overseeing the educational ministries of my former church. In the end, I agreed to become the chair of the department, and little did I know that this administrative assignment would become the first of many more to follow.

I came into academic leadership at a time of change—significant social and cultural change and unprecedented growth in Christian higher education. Yet virtually every provost and president I knew was a White male. There were a few female deans and department chairs, but the institution was predominantly White. There were even fewer faculty and staff of color across the university in any role, and there were virtually no Hispanic leaders anywhere to be found. And this was at a time when international students were coming to our campuses in high numbers, and students of color started enrolling at our institutions at an unprecedented rate. So on the one hand, the students were becoming more diverse; but on the other hand, the faculty and administration needed to keep pace. This was certainly the case in teacher education, where the students attending public and Christian schools in the greater Los Angeles metro region were from diverse ethnic and linguistic backgrounds. In contrast, those teaching them and those teaching the teachers were not from the same diverse backgrounds. Interestingly, I was the first Latino chair of the department and representative of the students my department was preparing teachers to teach.

Representative leadership carries an invisible weight of responsibility, like what my colleagues of color and I carried on the faculty. The pressure to carry an entire ethnic group upon one's shoulders is real and unsustainable. Fortunately, small gains have been made in the diversification of the faculty over the past three decades, but administrators of color continue to be seriously underrepresented. The absence of diverse administrators in Christian higher education is even more pronounced at the highest levels of administration—namely, as vice presidents and presidents. Regretfully, when I wrote this chapter, I was the only Latino president of a CCCU institution to my knowledge. Fortunately, the CCCU has recognized the need for the intentional development of leaders of color with the 2011 launch of the Multiethnic Leadership Development Institute (MELDI) and hosts a regular national Diversity Conference. I have been privileged to contribute to the content of both the MELDI and the Leadership Development Institute over the years, to serve as a resource leader and mentor for both, to present at the national Diversity Conference, and to serve as the first Senior Fellow for Diversity. Again, the gains have been modest, but they are gains nonetheless, and we need to remain intentional about developing leaders of color and Latinos for vice presidential and presidential roles.

A final word about navigating administration: serving in senior leadership can be incredibly rewarding. The opportunity to advance the Christian mission of an organization and shape its culture through operational decision-making, strategic planning, hiring, and budget allocation must be recognized. Senior leaders and presidents impact the organization for good in immeasurable ways, and administrative service is good work—it is essential work—and it generally pays well. It can also come at a cost. Unfortunately, the current higher education environment differs from what I experienced three decades ago.

The fallout of the COVID-19 pandemic continues to impact higher education negatively. This is most seen in declining enrollments, growing budget deficits, and staff and faculty layoffs due to organizational restructuring designed to ensure an institution's financial sustainability. Less visible are the stressors contributing to staff, faculty, and administrators leaving higher education altogether: burnout, general concern for physical health, and mental and emotional well-being. These are difficult times, and the Latino educator who aspires to administrative and institutional service must count the costs and be willing to drink the cup that Jesus drank (Matt. 20:22). Still, it can be done. Indeed, it must be done if our Christian higher education institutions are to have a future.

OUR STORIES MATTER

BENJAMIN D. ESPINOZA

Our stories matter. They help us make sense of our own experiences and the world around us, and they enable us to chart a path forward through trial and tribulation and joy and triumph. In this volume, we have sought to illuminate the stories of *nuestra gente* (our people). Our stories are diverse. They are each filled with their fair share of grief and difficulty but also joy and liberation. Our people are finding ways to survive and thrive in Christian higher education, and we are thrilled that we have had the opportunity to bring together the voices of beloved brothers and sisters.

I have come to this volume a little differently than my coeditor, Octavio. I am relatively new to academic life. Originally called to serve as a pastor, I sensed a strong desire to engage in the life of the mind through academia. I was able to research and write several articles and book reviews during my time in seminary, and I began attending and presenting at academic conferences. Even while I served as a pastor, I still engaged in scholarly activities and enjoyed the dialogue between what I was writing and reading and what I was doing in ministry.

At the beginning of my PhD program in higher, adult, and lifelong education, I was originally interested in adult learning and spirituality. However, within the first couple of months of the program, I realized that I wanted to study more about race and diversity. One of the first assignments I had to complete as a PhD student was to put together a research proposal. Instead of selecting a topic related to adult learning and spirituality, I developed a research proposal exploring the experiences of racially and ethnically minoritized doctoral students in evangelical theological institutions. I did so because the topic interested me and I honestly did not know much about that literature. In a conversation with my professor (coincidentally, the first Latina teacher or professor I had ever had), we came to the conclusion that I really wanted to study this topic because I was interested in understanding my own experiences as a Mexican American man in the United States.

I have always been proud of my Mexican heritage, but because I have light skin, people often perceive me as being a White male. Growing up, this certainly caused an identity crisis. Was I a Mexican, or was I simply a White man with Mexican heritage? Many of my friends understood my own Mexican heritage, but I still struggled with it. I do not speak fluent Spanish, nor did I grow up with all the customs and cultural practices that many of my Latine brothers and sisters did. Still, because of the influence of my grandmother, a leader in the Mexican American community in Detroit, I was brought up embracing my Mexican heritage.

Throughout college and seminary, I honestly desired more interaction with the Latino community. However, the institutions I attended were predominantly White, and I had so few opportunities to develop community with other Latinos. It wasn't until my time in a PhD program that I began to develop my own network of Latina/o friends. I enrolled in the Chicano and Latino studies advanced certificate program, which provided me with the kind of friendship, camaraderie, and community that I didn't realize I needed. This new *familia* embraced me in such significant ways and contributed to my own emotional and mental well-being during this taxing season of graduate studies.

My interests in race and diversity, alongside my commitment to the gospel of Christ, intersected when it came time to choose a topic for my dissertation. I had devoured the small but growing literature on Hispanic faculty in theological education. This topic became of great importance to me because I aspired to work in theological education but understood that there would be challenges there as a Latino male. In my dissertation, I ended up exploring the experiences of Hispanic faculty in evangelical theological education. My professors were incredibly supportive of this research endeavor, and I was so grateful to work with wonderful participants who honestly shared with me their journeys in evangelical theological education.

In the beginning of 2020, I landed my first academic role, an administrative one. I also taught courses on the side in the areas of ministry and leadership. Since that time, however, my career has been almost exclusively administrative in nature. Many of the struggles that my colleagues have shared here, I also share and deeply feel.

I share these small snippets of my own story because I want to express my deepest appreciation for the *hermanos* and *hermanas* who have generously shared their stories with Octavio and myself and, now, with you. Generally when somebody coedits a volume, they do so because they have a deep interest in the topic at hand and want to bring a multiplicity of perspectives together. But to be honest, another motivation of mine was that I could be inspired by the stories that my brothers and sisters have told here. As a young Latino male who anticipates spending a lifetime in Christian organizations, I need to hear stories of people who have found ways to survive and thrive in these often isolating, marginalizing, and exclusionary environments. Now don't get me wrong; there is so much that I love about Christian higher education and its ability to transform the lives of students so they can make a transformative impact on the world. But as we have seen in this volume, the struggles of our racially and ethnically minoritized brothers and sisters are very real in these institutions. The stories shared here inspire folks like myself, an emerging generation of Latino scholars and professors, to continue pursuing our dreams and creating spaces for others to thrive.

If there is any way to conclude this volume, it is to say that we must always pay attention to the lives and experiences and stories of people in our midst. From the perspective of Latina/os, our stories often become homogenized—that is to say, there is a tendency for people to try to identify "the Latina/o experience" in Christian higher education. However, as this volume has shown, we are not a monolith. There's so much incredible diversity in our community that no two stories are truly the same. That is the beauty of sharing our stories; every one of us has a unique experience that is worthy of hearing and engaging with. As the number of Latina/os in this nation continues to grow, we must continue to create spaces where we can continue to share our stories.

Sharing our stories is important not only because of the ways in which we are able to give voice to perspectives of marginalized folks but also for people to have the opportunity to listen and seek to make change where change needs to happen. As leaders in Christian higher education, we have the responsibility to listen to the stories of others and make changes so that all can find a space to thrive. As a young leader, I can tell you that this is still difficult. It is hard to keep an organization moving forward while also remaining attentive to the stories of people that need to be heard. This is why volumes such as these that bring together important stories are so vital to our work as educators; it is too easy to hear stories, feel inspired for a short moment, and then continue moving forward business as usual. We always have room to improve!

As Octavio shared in the introduction, we are all on a journey, and we are glad you have journeyed with us through these stories from our beloved brothers and sisters. All journeys have their fair share of challenges and joys, yet we must remain diligent in our support of one another. To close, I offer the Romero Prayer, which has served as a foundational text in the life of my own institution. Named for Bishop Oscar Romero, but written by Bishop Ken Utener of Saginaw, the Romero Prayer is a reminder that the work ahead is incomplete. Yet we continue to move forward.

It helps, now and then, to step back and take a long view.
The kingdom is not only beyond our efforts, it is even beyond our vision.
We accomplish in our lifetime only a tiny fraction of the magnificent
enterprise that is God's work. Nothing we do is complete, which is a way of
saying that the Kingdom always lies beyond us.
No statement says all that could be said.
No prayer fully expresses our faith.
No confession brings perfection.
No pastoral visit brings wholeness.
No program accomplishes the Church's mission.
No set of goals and objectives includes everything.
This is what we are about.
We plant the seeds that one day will grow.
We water seeds already planted, knowing that they hold future promise.
We lay foundations that will need further development.
We provide yeast that produces far beyond our capabilities.
We cannot do everything, and there is a sense of liberation in realizing that.

This enables us to do something, and to do it very well.

It may be incomplete, but it is a beginning, a step along the way, an opportunity for the Lord's grace to enter and do the rest.

We may never see the end results, but that is the difference between the master builder and the worker.

We are workers, not master builders; ministers, not messiahs.

We are prophets of a future not our own.

Adelante, friends. *Adelante.*

Contributors

Octavio Javier Esqueda is a full professor of Christian higher education and director of the PhD and EdD programs in educational studies at the Talbot School of Theology at Biola University. He graduated from the University of Guadalajara, Dallas Theological Seminary, and the University of North Texas, where he earned a PhD in higher education. Dr. Esqueda has several publications on theological education, Christian higher education, and literature, including the coauthored books *Anointed Teaching: Partnership with the Holy Spirit* and *The Cruciform Faculty: The Making of a Christian Professor*. He is an academic leader and practical theologian with worldwide experience and is an avid soccer fan.

Benjamin Dallas Espinoza served as vice president of Northeastern Seminary at Roberts Wesleyan University in Rochester, New York. He previously served as special advisor to the president for diversity and belonging, associate vice president of adult and online education, and executive director of seminary administration. He is a graduate of Cedarville University, Asbury Theological Seminary, and Michigan State University, where he earned his PhD in higher, adult, and lifelong education. He is the editor of *Theology and the Star Wars Universe* and lead editor of *Story, Formation, and Culture: From Theory to Practice in Ministry with Children*. Ben has written numerous articles in the areas of Christian formation and ministry, race and diversity, theological education, and leadership.

Leticia I. Espinoza is originally from México. She arrived in Grand Rapids to finish her engineering degree in 1998; instead, she graduated from Calvin College with a major in business/communications and a minor in English. Later she received her doctorate in Hispanic works of literature from Western Michigan University. At Hope College, she teaches language and literature.

Michael Jimenez earned his PhD from Fuller Theological Seminary and is an associate professor of history at Vanguard University. He is the author of *Remembering Lived Lives: A Historiography from the Underside of Modernity* and *Karl Barth and the Study of the Religious Enlightenment: Encountering the Task of History*. He is currently researching the influence of Cesar Chavez's nonviolent activism and the recent history of Costa Rica.

Itzel Meduri Soto is a daughter of Mexican immigrants, born and raised in Los Angeles, California. She is a graduate of Los Angeles Harbor College; California State University, Dominguez Hills; and the University of California, Irvine. She is currently an associate professor of Spanish at Biola University, where she teaches second language and heritage language learners. Her writings cover a wide range of subjects, including bilingualism, racial identity, immigration, and mothering.

A son of Puerto Rico and the US South, **Nathan Luis Cartagena** was born in Charleston, South Carolina, and raised in Somerset, New Jersey. He is an Assistant Professor of Philosophy at Wheaton College (IL), where he teaches courses on race, justice, and political philosophy. He is a fellow in The Wheaton Center for Early Christian Studies and is an affiliate faculty member in the Latin American and Latino/a studies program.

Verónica A. Gutiérrez is a historian specializing in the origins of Mexican Catholicism, is the director of the Great Books program en español for the Angelicum Academy, a Catholic homeschooling program renowned for its online Socratic discussions, as well as a History Faculty Fellow for Hildegard College. A trained writer, award-winning scholar, and sought-after speaker, she has provided keynotes in the United States and México; co-led a faculty development tour through México; given a TEDx talk about Cholula, Puebla, México; and published in English and Spanish. Her scholarship and teaching challenge the myths pervading native peoples of the Americas. She is writing a children's chapter book for Ignatius Press about sixteenth-century native visionary Juan Diego, relating this well-known story from an Indigenous perspective, thereby introducing readers to the beauties of Nahua culture and the Nahuatl (Aztec) language.

Damon A. Horton is the program director of intercultural studies and an assistant professor at California Baptist University. He received his PhD in applied theology from Southeastern Baptist Theological Seminary, emphasizing North American missions. His dissertation was titled *The Qualitative and Quantitative Measuring of Spiritual Capital among Latinas/os in Higher Education*. He is currently coediting two academic works intersecting Christianity and justice, and his research interests include the Community Cultural Wealth model, Latin American missiology, and urban apologetics. He has been married to Elicia for twenty years, and they have three children. He and Elicia serve on staff at the Grove Community Church.

Pete C. Menjares is an author and higher education professional with three decades of experience. Dr. Menjares is a two-time university president, a provost and senior vice president, a professor, and a trustee. Dr. Menjares most recently served as the interim president and member of the Board of Seattle Pacific University (Seattle, WA). Prior to this assignment, Dr. Menjares served as provost and senior vice president for academic affairs at Vanguard University (Costa Mesa, CA), the eleventh president of Fresno Pacific University (Fresno, CA), and a professor and administrator at Biola University (La Mirada, CA), where he held the positions of associate professor of education, education department chair, associate provost for diversity leadership, and vice provost for faculty development and academic effectiveness. He is a Senior Fellow for Diversity with the Council for Christian Colleges and Universities (Washington, DC).